Anonymus

Records of the Australian Museum

Anonymus

Records of the Australian Museum

ISBN/EAN: 9783742858887

Manufactured in Europe, USA, Canada, Australia, Japa

Cover: Foto ©Thomas Meinert / pixelio.de

Manufactured and distributed by brebook publishing software
(www.brebook.com)

Anonymus

Records of the Australian Museum

RECORDS

OF THE

AUSTRALIAN MUSEUM

EDITED BY THE CURATOR.

Vol. II.

PRINTED BY ORDER OF THE TRUSTEES

E. P. RAMSAY, LL.D.,

SUCCEEDED BY

R. ETHERIDGE, JUNR.,

Curator.

SYDNEY, 1892-96.

CONTENTS.

———:o:———

No. 5. Published September, 1893.
Pages 55-84. Plates xii.-xvii.

No. 6. Published September, 1895.
Pages 85-94. Plates xviii.-xxii.

No. 7. Published January, 1896.
Pages i.-xii., 95-112. Plate xxiii.

LIST OF THE CONTRIBUTORS.

With References to the Articles contributed by each.

————:o:————

LIST OF PLATES.

CORRECTIONS.

Page 91, line 17, read p. 35 instead of p. 1.

Explanation of plate xiii. fig. 2, read fig. 1 instead of fig. 2.

,,   ,,   ,, 3, read figs. 1 and 2, instead of figs. 2 and 3.

On a TUBICOLOUS AMPHIPOD from PORT JACKSON.

By Chas. Chilton, M.A., B.Sc.

[With Plate I.]

AMONG some Australian Crustacea sent me as exchanges by the Trustees of the Australian Museum was a tube-dwelling Amphipod collected in Port Jackson. There was a plentiful supply both of specimens and of the tubes formed by them and after a full examination and comparison of them with Mr. Stebbing's description and figures I have no doubt that they belong to *Cerapus flindersi*, Stebbing,[*] a species described from a single female specimen taken in Flinder's Passage during the voyage of the "Challenger." Mr. Stebbing says nothing of the tube in his description, and I presume therefore, that he has not seen it. I am now able to supplement his description in this respect and also to describe the male of the species, and to give the points in which it differs from the female, and also some interesting facts on the changes in form that occur during the growth of the male.

The genus *Cerapus* was originally established in 1817 by Say, and the species *Cerapus tubularis* was afterwards fully redescribed in 1880 by S. I. Smith who established for it a new sub-family *Cerapinæ* in the family *Corophiidæ*.[†] He thus describes the new sub-family :—

"The single known genus differs from the *Podocerinæ* and allied groups in the following characters. There are only three pairs of branchial lamellæ, which are borne on the third, fourth and fifth segments of the peræon, and only three pairs of ovigerous lamellæ, which are borne on the second, third, and fourth segments. The second and third pleopods are much smaller than the first, and their inner lamellæ are rudimentary or very small. The second and third uropods are uniramous and nearly alike, the distal extremity in each being short and terminating in a hooked joint.

"The only known species inhabits unattached, portable tubes, and, as in many allied genera, has large cement glands in the bases of the first and second peræopods."

The above quotation has been taken from Stebbing's "Report on the "Challenger" Amphipoda," as I am unable to consult Professor Smith's original paper. I am therefore unable, also, to compare the present species in detail with *Cerapus tubularis*, Say. The "cement glands" in the first and second peræopods have been

---

[*] Report on the "Challenger" Amphipoda, p. 1163, plate cxxv.
[†] See Stebbing's Report of the "Challenger" Amphipoda, p. 522.

A

very fully investigated by Nebeski,[*] but for this reference again I am indebted to Stebbing's report.

In addition to our present species Stebbing has described another new species *Cerapus sismithi*, taken during the Challenger Expedition at Kerguelen Island.[†]

In the following detailed description of the various parts of the animal I have omitted all those parts where I had nothing to add to Mr. Stebbing's description.

Head and body.—The head is produced anteriorly into a subacute rostrum between the bases of the antennæ, much in the same way as is shown in Mr. Stebbing's figure of *Cerapus sismithi*, but in none of my specimens have I noticed the rostrum to be "carinate" as it is drawn and described by Mr. Stebbing in *C. flindersi*. (See figures A and B.)

The relative lengths of the various segments of the percion of the female agree well with Stebbing's description, but in the male they are quite different. In this (see fig. B.) the first segment is about as long as the head, the second is slightly longer, anteriorly it is slightly narrower than the first segment, but about the middle it suddenly widens to twice this width thus giving attachment to the large and powerful second gnathopoda ; the third segment is considerably shorter than the second and is also narrower anteriorly but it widens posteriorly ; the fourth is shorter again than the third, as wide anteriorly, but narrowing posteriorly ; the fifth segment which is so long in the female, is only a little longer than the fourth and not so long as the third ; the sixth is subequal to the fifth in length and breadth ; the seventh is as broad but shorter.

Upper Antennæ.—These agree on the whole with Stebbing's description, but the first joint of the peduncle is not "much longer than the second joint"; it is usually about the same length and in large specimens may even be somewhat shorter. The flagellum may contain as many as seven joints, usually there are more than four, the number given in Stebbing's description. (See fig. a. s.)

Lower Antennæ.—These also differ in a few details. The fourth joint is not "dilated at the base," nor "abruptly broader than the preceding joint" in any of the specimens that I have examined, indeed the fourth joint is usually narrowed a little at the base and it articulates with only a portion of the end of the third joint so that the articulation is not very strong and the fourth joint is very freely movable upon the third. (See fig. a. i.)

---

* " Beitrage zur Kentniss der Amphipoden der Adria"—Arb. Zool. Inst. Wien. Bd. III.   (See Stebbing's Report on the "Challenger" Amphipoda, p. 518.)

† Report on the "Challenger" Amphipoda, p. 1158, Pl. cxxiv.

TUBICOLOUS AMPHIPOD—CHILTON.

In large sized males the lower antennæ are stouter and more pediform than in younger specimens, and the long setæ are by no means so conspicuous.

The mouth parts appear to correspond closely with Stebbing's description, but I have not examined them in great detail.

The first gnathopoda are the same in both sexes and agree with Stebbing's description as closely as can be expected when allowance is made for individual variation.

The second gnathopoda differ very much in the two sexes. In the female they do not differ very greatly from the first gnathopoda and agree very closely with the description already given by Mr. Stebbing. I give a drawing for the sake of comparison with the second gnathopoda of the male, (see fig. *gn. 2 ♀*). In the male the second gnathopoda differ considerably from those of the female and also differ very much at different stages in the development of the same individual. The form most commonly met with is that shown in fig. *gn. 2 ♂ B*, which represents the second gnathopod of a moderate sized male; it will be convenient to describe this first.

The first free joint, the *basos*, is narrow at the base where it articulates with the moderate sized side-plate but rapidly widens until at the widest part it is more than half as broad as long; the anterior edge is straight except near the base and is fringed with about ten spinules, the posterior margin is strongly convex and bears two or three setæ at the apex; the *ischios* and the *meros* are of the usual shape and not unlike those of the female; the meros has the distal extremity produced, rounded and tipped with a few setæ; the carpus is very large and broad, its anterior margin very convex especially towards the base, a small group of setæ* at its distal extremity, the posterior margin is indistinctly serrate and bears five groups of long setæ in the serrations, other shorter setæ are situated between the serrations and a few on the surface of the joint; the postero-distal corner is produced acutely and reaches about half way along the inner margin of the propodos, and between this corner and the inner articulation of the propodos is a short rounded lobe reaching only about half as far. The *propodos* is considerably shorter than the carpus, rather more than twice as long as broad, the anterior margin curved and bearing about six spinules, that at the apex the longest; the posterior margin with the basal half smooth, but the distal half minutely serrate or more strictly speaking crenate, the whole margin fringed with abundant long setæ, a few others being situated along the surface of the joint; the *dactylos* is like that of the female and has the inner margin denticulate towards the distal end, but the inner margin of the terminal tooth again is smooth.

---

* These serrations are not shown very distinctly in the plate.

In one large and evidently old male, about ½ inch in length, the second gnathopod was much elongated and at first sight appeared very different.   A close comparison shows however that it is simply a more developed form of the gnathopod just described, and that the two are not dimorphic forms.   The whole limb is much elongated and the setæ are fewer and much smaller in proportion ; this loss of setæ was also noticeable in the antennæ and I have noticed examples in several other species which seem to show that it is a change that very generally accompanies age and increase of growth.

The side-plates (*epimera*), (see fig. *gn. 2 ♂ A*) are small and are produced anteriorly into a moderately acute process which bears two or three setæ ; the basos is of the same general shape as that found in the younger male but is much narrower, the ischios and meros are also similar but more elongated and the setæ at the end of the meros are very few and small ; the carpus is immensely elongated and consequently much narrower in proportion, it is narrow towards the base and widens again distally, the anterior margin is quite free from setæ except one or two very small ones at the apex, the posterior margin is straight with five distinct serrations, in each of which are two or three short setæ ; the extremity is produced into two long processes about half as long as the propodos, the process formed of the postero-distal corner having the sides parallel and the end truncate, the other, corresponding to the small rounded lobe in the younger male, with the outer margin straight, inner margin slightly concave, extremity rounded, quite free from setæ ; the propodos is very long and narrow, the breadth not more than one-fifth the total length, the whole joint is much curved inwards, the inner margin being very concave and fringed with a row of scattered setæ ; the finger is stouter and blunter than in the younger male and has the inner margin smooth.   The propodos is not movable quite in the same plane as that of the carpus, but bends back on one side of it so as to lie obliquely along its surface.

I have seen only one very large male with the second gnathopoda like that shown in fig. *gn. 2 ♂ A.*   Most of them were more like the one represented in fig. *gn. 2 ♂ B*, but in some the two processes at the end of the carpus were a little more developed, in others a little less developed than those shown in this figure. Forms younger still than that represented in fig. *gn. 2 ♂ B* would no doubt approximate more closely to the female in the form of second gnathopoda.

The first perciopoda agree closely with the description given by Stebbing, but I have not observed the "long transverse slit" across the surface of the basos that he mentions.

The second perciopoda also closely resemble Stebbing's description.   In both this and the preceding pair the side plates are produced anteriorly into a small rounded lobe tipped with setæ, that of the first pair being considerably larger than that of the second.

The third pereiopoda have the side plates very large, delicate and membranaceous. Those of the female are very much larger than those of the male, a fact which tends to confirm Mr. Stebbing's supposition that they fulfil the function of marsupial plates. The side plates extend along the whole segment forming a small lobe in the rear and are of about uniform depth, the two lower corners being broadly rounded, the lower margin being usually slightly concave in the middle. The margin is somewhat uneven, entire or irregularly crenate, and is irregularly fringed with setæ. The rest of the limb is attached to the side plate at the rear and usually projects directly backwards. The relative sizes of the side plates as compared with the rest of the limb in the two sexes can be seen by comparing figures *prp. 3 ♂* and *prp. 3 ♀*. The other joints of the limb are practically identical in the two sexes and agree closely with Stebbing's description.

The fourth pereiopoda have the branchial vesicles very small, narrow and bent at the base. The whole limb is much as described by Stebbing, but is usually provided with fewer setæ ; the lower margin of the side plates is thickly fringed with cilia in the male, but these are very delicate and I have failed to find them in some other specimens.

The fifth pereiopoda and the *pleopoda* agree with Stebbing's description and do not call for special remark.

The uropoda which are represented in the figure as seen from above, agree with Stebbing's description, the third pair however being very much broader in proportion to the length than the second pair. (See fig, *ur. 1* &c.)

The telson when seen from above proves to be bi-lobed as in *Cerapus sismithi*, the dividing cleft extending about half way towards the base, each lobe rounded and bearing on the surface two rows of sharp upturned teeth.

Locality.—Port Jackson, New South Wales.

Remarks.—The whole integument of the hinder portion of the body with the appendages is very thin and delicate, membranaceous. The animal rests in the tube with the head and first segment of the pereion and usually the ends of the second gnathopoda projecting out at the end (see fig. A) and the pleon is bent back upon the body as shown in figure B. Doubtless the sharp teeth, setæ, and serrations on the uropoda and the telson enable the animal to fix this portion of the body to the inner surface of the tube, and by extending the body and again bringing up the pleon to its reflexed position to push its way along the tube.*

The tube (see fig. A) is cylindrical, of the same diameter throughout except at each end where it is somewhat widened ; the two ends are quite similar and appear to be equally and indifferently used by the animal. The tube is quite free and unattached and is no doubt carried about by the animal when it moves. The material of which it is made is fairly tough, the surface is smooth and the whole appears to be formed from the secretion produced by the glands in the first and second pereiopoda, no sand grains being used as in *Cerapus sismithi*.

The tubes that I have seen are all of the same shape, but they very much in size, the largest being about ·46 inches long and ·03 inches in diameter, others being of only half these dimensions. Many of the tubes and especially of the smaller ones were empty and I presume that when the animal has grown too large for its tube it leaves it and secretes another and larger one.

From the description which has now been given of the male of this species it appears that *C. flindersi* is not very different from *C. sismithi* described by Stebbing from Kerguelen Island ; it differs from that species however in the antennæ, to some extent in the second gnathopoda and also in the armature of the uropoda.

DESCRIPTIONS OF THREE NEW AUSTRALIAN LIZARDS.

By J. Douglas Ogilby.

1. GYMNODACTYLUS SPHYRURUS, *sp. nov.*

Head rather large ; a strong transverse ridge crosses the occiput immediately behind the eyes, ending on either side in a blunt point placed at the postero-superior angle of the orbit ; from this runs forward an inwardly curved, elevated, supraciliary ridge which is continued on the snout by a conversely curved angular canthus rostralis ; these ridges form the margin on the forehead of an oval, and between the orbits of a subtriangular, depression; loreal region concave ; the length of the snout is one and two-fifths

---

* Some very interesting remarks on *Cerapus abditus* were given many years ago by Templeton, see Stebbing's " Report on the ' Challenger ' Amphipoda," p. 168.

of the diameter of the eye, and the distance between the eye and the ear-opening is equal to that between the eye and a point midway between the nostril and the tip of the snout. Interorbital space broad, broader in comparison than in *G. platurus* or *G. cornutus*. Ear-opening a narrow vertical slit, about one-third of the diameter of the eye. Body short and rather compressed, barely two and a third times the length of the head. Limbs long; digits rather short and thick, subcylindrical at the base, and but little compressed on the distal phalanges. Head covered with small granules intermixed with rounded tubercles, which are largest near the end of the snout; outer margin of the upper eyelid with two strong ridges upon which small tubercles predominate; two slight longitudinal folds on the sides of the neck and a vertical fold in front of the forelimb, all of which are more thickly studded with tubercles than are the surrounding parts; rostral hexagonal twice as broad as high, without any indication of median groove above; nostril directed posteriorly, bordered in front by a large nasal, which is larger than the first upper labial, and separated from the latter by a series of small granules; labials small, thirteen or fourteen upper and eleven lower; mental trapezoidal, bordered posteriorly by five small granules; body above covered by minute granules, intermixed with rounded and conical tubercles; limbs similarly protected, but with the granules larger and the tubercles smaller; below with flat subimbricate granules; no lateral fold. Tail short, broad, and thick, depressed, malleiform, not contracted at the base, from which the enlarged portion expands at right angles; the expanded portion is formed of six broad transverse ridges, and is quadrilateral; its length is three-fourths of its breadth, which is one-sixth more than that of the body at its broadest part; it ends almost as abruptly as it commences, and terminates in an attenuated point, which rises from the postero-inferior margin of the swollen portion, and is barely four-sevenths of its length; the tail is covered above by minute granules anteriorly and much larger flattened subimbricate granules posteriorly; on the former portion there are four regular transverse series of strong conical tubercles, on the latter a single series on each side near the margin; sides with an upper series of very strong conical tubercles, and a lower series of weaker ones; below with subimbricate granules; attenuated portion covered with small rounded granules.

Colors.—Head and neck above brown with darker and lighter marbling and most of the tubercles yellow; the sides pale yellowish-brown with irregular blackish bands, which are vertical on the former and horizontal on the latter; back brown with narrow yellowish transverse bands, mainly caused by the prevalence of that color on the tubercles; sides and limbs light brown streaked and marbled with darker brown; under surface dirty yellowish-

brown ; tail above dark brown, the expanded portion with two
broad light colored cross-bands ; the anterior near its commence-
ment, the posterior marking its termination ; below dark brown
densely spotted with yellow ; the attenuated portion with two
annular yellow rings.

Dimensions.

Total length	89	millim.
Length of head	18	,,
Width of head	13	,,
Length of body	42	,,
Length of fore limb ...	24	,,
Length of hind limb ...	30	,,
Length of tail	29	,,

Habitat.—Interior of New South Wales (Tumut?).

Type.—In the Australian Museum, Sydney.

The unique example described above forms one of a small collection lately forwarded to the Museum. The bottle which contained it is labelled "Tumut," but as the remaining bottles are
unlabelled, and no information as to the sender is procurable,
some doubt as to the true locality necessarily remains.

This species differs greatly from the other broad-tailed forms
of *Gymnodactylus*, but is more closely allied to *G. miliusii*, than
to *platurus* or *cornutus*.

2. GYMNODACTYLUS CORNUTUS, *sp. nov.*

Head large, the snout depressed, the occiput raised above the
level of the eye and forming with the snout a moderately convex
surface the apical point of which is on a line with the posterior
margin of the orbit ; the length of the snout is one and three-
fourths of the diameter of the eye ; the distance between the eye
and the nostril is greater than that between the eye and the ear-
opening. Forehead and loreal region slightly concave ; supraciliary region so much enlarged and elevated as to leave only a
deep narrow fossa between the orbits. Ear-opening elongate-
pyriform, vertical, five-eighths of the diameter of the eye. Body
moderately elongate and attenuated, more than three and a half
times the length of the head. Limbs long ; digits strong, subcylindrical at the base, the distal portion strongly compressed and
elevated ; claws very strong. Head covered with small granules
intermixed with conical or rounded tubercles ; granules of the
upper eyelid rather larger than those of the head, the tubercles
numerous and rounded ; a strong spinate knob, surmounted by a
conical tubercle behind the eye ; ear-opening protected in front
and above by a tuberculated ridge ; rostral subquadrangular,
three times as broad as high, almost completely divided by a
shallow median groove ; nostril directed posteriorly, in contact

with the rostral and first labial; labials small, fifteen upper and thirteen lower; mental trapezoidal, bordered posteriorly by five enlarged granules. An arcuate row of six strong conical tubercles, each of which is encircled by smaller tubercles, on the nuchal region; body and limbs above covered with small granules, intermixed with rounded, conical, and spinose tubercles; below with flat granules; the two separated by a very distinct flap, the outer margin of which is ornamented with a series of triangular dermal appendages, each of which is provided with a similar smaller appendage in front and behind. Tail of moderate length, depressed, broad, leaf-like, strongly contracted at the base, and attenuated at the tip, covered above by minute granular scales, intermixed, except on a vertebral patch of the leaf-like expansion, with soft triangular appendages.

Colors.—Chestnut- or blackish-brown above, with five large angular whitish spots, undulated or marbled with brown, the first and smallest on the nuchal region, the fifth between the hind limbs; a whitish band from behind the eye to the ear-opening, and another along the side of the neck immediately in front of the fore limb; labials white, marbled with dark brown; limbs above with indications of lighter cross-bars; tail with three broad whitish transverse bands above; below white, uniform or minutely spotted with brown.

Dimensions.

Total length	...	210 millim.
Length of head	...	37 "
Width of head	...	31 "
Length of body	...	90 "
Length of fore limb	...	66 "
Length of hind limb	...	72 "
Length of tail	...	83 "

Habitat.—Bellenden-Ker Ranges, North-eastern Queensland.

Type.—In the Australian Museum, Sydney.

The first examples of this fine Gecko which came under my notice formed part of a collection obtained by Messrs. Cairn and Grant during the autumn of 1889 in the locality indicated above; these were determined, on a cursory examination, as "*Gymnodactylus platurus*, northern form" (vide Rec. Austr. Mus. i. p. 30). A fine example since forwarded, with other material, to the Museum by Mr. Day, coupled with the fact that at the time of its arrival I was engaged on a revision of the Australian Geckos, induced me to pay more attention to this form, with the result that I find it to be very distinct from *G. platurus*, its nearest ally, with which it has evidently been confounded, and which also ranges at least as far northwards as the Bellenden-Ker one of the specimens collected by Messrs. Cairn and Grant being specifically inseparable from the southern Leaf-tailed Gecko.

Five out of the six specimens available for examination had reproduced tails, that of the remaining example being as described above; whether this lepidosis is normal or abnormal is, under the circumstances, rather a difficult question to decide, but the fact that I have before me an example of *Gymnodactylus platurus* which though fully adult and with a longer and more attenuated tail than prevails in the ordinary run of specimens, has this vertebral patch as fully developed as in the specimen described; it seems, therefore, probable that this locally unarmed patch may or may not be present in individuals of the same species, since other undoubted specimens of *G. platurus* show little or no sign of it.

3. DIPLODACTYLUS INTERMEDIUS, *sp. nov.*

Head oviform, convex; snout rounded, much longer than the distance between the eye and the ear-opening, from once and three-fourths to twice the diameter of the orbit; eye large; ear-opening of moderate size, round. Body and limbs rather strong. Digits depressed, with large transverse lamellæ inferiorly, seven or eight under the fourth toe, the two or three anterior subcordiform, the middle two transversely oblong, and the basal ones divided into two subcircular plates; the plates under the apex of the digits large, together cordiform. Upper surfaces covered with moderate-sized, juxtaposed, round or oval granules, distinctly smaller on the nuchal region intermixed on the back with large conical tubercles, forming two regular longitudinal series, which extend a short distance along the tail. Rostral subquadrangular, completely divided mesially; nostril pierced between the rostral, first labial, and three nasals, the anterior of which is much the larger, and is separated from its fellow by a transverse oval granule, which is rarely split in two; eleven to thirteen upper and ten to twelve lower labials; mental small, triangular or trapezoidal, not or but little larger than the adjacent labials; no regular chin-shields. Lower surfaces covered with small juxtaposed granules largest on the chin, smallest on the throat. Males with a curved series of preanal pores, five or six on each side, interrupted in the middle, and with from two to four large granules on each side of the base of the tail. Tail short, subcylindrical, covered with small granules; seventeen more or less regular transverse bands of strong tubercles, the anterior band connecting the terminal points of the dorsal and basi-caudal longitudinal series.

Colors.—Upper surfaces bluish-gray, with irregular lines and patches of black scales; all the tubercles yellow; lower surfaces gray, closely dotted with black or brown, each dot representing a granule.

Dimensions.

Total length	...	...	100 millim.
Length of head	...	...	16 ,,
Width of head	...	...	11·5 ,,
Body	..	...	.. 47 ,,
Fore limb	...	...	... 22·5 ,,
Hind limb	...	...	27 ,,
Tail	...	...	... 57 ,,

Habitat.—Interior of New South Wales.

The species here described belongs to the tuberculated section of the genus, but differs in several constant characters from each of the three described forms belonging to that section ; from *ciliaris* it is manifestly different in the absence of spinous tubercles on the supraciliary region, while from *strophurus* it is equally well distinguished by the presence of tubercles on the tail ; its nearest ally, therefore, is *spinigerus*, whose place it would appear to take in the interior of this Colony ; from that species, however, it differs in the following, among other, characters :—The snout is very much longer; the dorsal tubercles form two regular longitudinal series ; there are eleven to thirteen upper and ten to twelve lower labials only ; and the tail is armed with transverse rows of strong tubercles ; while in *spinigerus* the snout is only a little longer than the diameter of the orbit, the tubercles are irregularly scattered over the dorsal surface, there are thirteen to fifteen upper, and as many lower labials, and the caudal tubercles are arranged in a single longitudinal series on each side of the tail and are black.

SUPPLEMENT to the DESCRIPTIVE CATALOGUE of "NESTS and EGGS of BIRDS FOUND BREEDING in AUSTRALIA and TASMANIA."
[Part II., April 1892.]
By A. J. NORTH, F.L.S.

Since the issue of Part I. the following new nests and eggs have been obtained and are herein described :—*Edoliisoma tenuirostre, Turnix melanotus, Ptilotis frenata,* and *Polytelis alexandrae.* Descriptions of nests and eggs also appear that are not given in the Catalogue, as well as additional information on the nidification of other species. I here express my indebtedness to the collectors or correspondents from whom the specimens were obtained and whose names will be found prefixed to each description.

FALCO MELANOGENYS, *Gould.*   Black-cheeked Falcon.

Gould, Handbk. Bds. Austr., Vol. i., sp. 8, p. 26.

Regarding the additional information on the breeding habits of *Falco melanogenys,* the most courageous of all our Raptorial birds, I am indebted to Dr. L. Holden, of Circular Head, and Mr. E. D. Atkinson, of Table Cape, North-west Tasmania. From the former gentleman's notes kindly sent me I have extracted the following :—

"On the 10th of September, 1887, Mr. E. D. Atkinson, took two fresh eggs of this species on a ledge of cliffs between Sister's Hill and Boat Harbour." "On the 4th of October, 1888, I found a nesting place of the Black-cheeked Falcon on the cliffs that bound Sister's Beach on the South-east, it was the same place that Mr. Atkinson obtained his nest on the 10th of September, 1887. The eggs were three in number and hard set, but could be blown, and laid on the rock without any nest, the ledge being but some ten or twelve feet from the base of the cliff, and was quite easily reached by a zigzag approach scarcely to be called a climb, the projecting rocks forming an easy stairway." Dr. Holden visited the same place on the 26th of September, 1889, but there were no eggs. On the 30th of September, 1891, he writes as follows :—"I took a clutch of Falcon's eggs last Saturday, the 26th inst., from the same spot to an inch which I robbed in 1888. It is not bare rock where the eggs were found, there is a covering of grit and detritus. In more frequented spots these birds take care to breed in as inaccessible places as possible, and although in Tasmania the Black-cheeked Falcons are numerous, their eggs are usually unattainable."

The above set of eggs are typical eggs of this species, they are in form rounded ovals, the isabelline ground colour of which is almost obscured by minute freckles, dots, spots, and irregular shaped blotches of deep reddish-brown ; in one instance these markings are evenly dispersed over the surface of the shell, in the others they become confluent, forming a cap on the larger end in one specimen, and on the smaller end in another. Length (A) 2·12 x 1·65 inch ; (B) 2·17 x 1·65 inch ; (C) 2·18 x 1·67 inch.

This bird usually breeds on the rocky cliffs of the coast in the vicinity of which it is more frequently found, but the late Mr. Kenric Harold Bennett obtained the eggs of this Falcon for several seasons on Mt. Manara, an isolated rocky prominence rising out of a plain in the Western District of New South Wales.

In favourable situations, with the exception of the Northern and North-eastern portions of the Continent, this species is found all over Australia.

STRIX CANDIDA, *Tickell.*   Grass Owl.

Gould, Suppl. Bds. Austr., fol. edit., pl. i.

Mr. J. A. Boyd, of the Herbert River, Queensland, has kindly sent the following notes relative to the nidification of this species: "This Owl nests on the ground, choosing a high thick tussock of grass, forming a bower in it, and laying its eggs on the few grass blades that have been trampled down. On the 1st of June, 1884, I found two nests of this bird, each of which contained three young ones and one egg. It is a curious fact that though this bird always lays four eggs, I never found more than three young ones, one egg being always addled. A friend of mine here has also had the same experience. It seems strange that the bird should lay an egg more than she is able to hatch. When first I came here these birds were comparatively common, but latterly have almost disappeared from this immediate neighbourhood, owing I think to the largely increased quantity of cattle running over the plain."

The two eggs referred to by Mr. Boyd are more elongated than is the rule with most Owl's eggs, and may be described as thick ovals in form, white, the shell with the exception of a few calcareous excrescences at the larger end being perfectly smooth and lustreless. Length (A) 1·69 x 1·27 inch ; (B) 1·73 x 1·26 inch.

The range of this species extends over India, China, the Phillipine Islands, and the Northern and Eastern portions of Australia.

EDOLIISOMA TENUIROSTRE, *Jardine.*   Jardine's Campephaga.

Graucalus tenuirostris, Jard., Edinb. Journ. Nat. Sci. iv. p. 211.
Ceblepyris jardinii, Rüppell, Mus. Senckenb. iii. p. 30.
Campephaga jardinii, Gould, Bds. Austr. fol. Vol. ii. pl. 60.

Gould, Handbk. Bds. Austr., Vol. i., sp. 109, p. 200.

*During the latter end of September, 1882, Mr. C. C. L. Talbot observed a pair of these birds building their nest in the angle of a thin forked horizontal branch of an Ironbark (*Eucalyptus sp.*), about forty feet from the ground, on Collaroy Station, Broad Sound, 556 miles N.W. of Brisbane. A week after, seeing the female sitting on the nest for some length of time, he climbed up to it and found it contained a perfectly fresh egg, which he took (not waiting for the full complement, which is probably two), as the tree was a difficult one to climb, at the same time securing the nest. It was a small and shallow structure composed of wiry grasses securely fastened together with cobwebs, and closely resembled the branch on which it was placed. The egg is ovoid in form, of a very pale bluish-grey ground colour, uniformly

* North, Rec. Austr. Mus., Vol. i., No. 8, July, 1891.

spotted and dotted with irregular shaped markings of different shades of umber and slaty-brown, underlying blotches of slaty-grey appearing as if beneath the surface of the shell. Length 1·2 x 0·82 inch. In the colour and disposition of its markings, it resembles some varieties of the eggs of *Sittella chrysoptera*, and in shape and size that of the egg of *Graucalus hyperleucus*, but is entirely free from the asparagus-green ground colour which predominates in the eggs of the latter genus. This is the only occasion I have known of the nest and egg of this species having been taken.

The Northern and Eastern portions of the Australian Continent constitutes the habitat of this species.

CHIBIA BRACTEATA, *Gould.* Spangled Drongo-Shrike.

Gould, Handbk. Bds. Austr., Vol. i., sp. 132, p. 235.

This migratory species is rather freely dispersed over the greater portions of Northern and Eastern Australia, it arrives at Cape York about the middle of April, and the Herbert River in May. Mr. C. C. L. Talbot found it breeding on Collaroy Station, near Broad Sound, Queensland, on the 10th of October, 1882. The nests in every instance were open and slightly cup-shaped structures, composed entirely of long stems of a climbing plant and fibrous roots, and were attached to the fine leafy twigs at the extremities of the branches of a dwarf white gum, at an altitude of twenty feet from the ground. The nests were placed in trees about fifty yards apart, and in the twelve nests examined each of them contained three eggs for a sitting; in some the eggs were perfectly fresh, in others partly incubated, but none were found containing young ones. The eggs are oval in form, somewhat pointed at one end, and are of a very pale purplish-grey ground colour, with numerous scratches and irregular shaped markings of light reddish-purple, scattered over the entire surface of the shell, many of which are nearly obsolete. All the markings have a faded and washed out appearance, and the shell is dull and lustreless. A set measures, length (A) 1·2 x 0·83 inch; (B) 1·18 x 0·83 inch; (C) 1·23 x 0·85 inch.

BATHILDA RUFICAUDA, *Gould.* Red-tailed Finch.

Gould, Handbk. Bds. Austr., Vol. i., sp. 254, p. 412.

This pretty little Finch, although by no means common, has a most extensive range of habitat, being found throughout Northern, North-eastern and North-western Australia, it is also very sparingly dispersed over the Northern and Interior portions of New South Wales, but in the latter districts it is considered a rare species, being very seldom obtained; a small flock was seen near Lithgow in the Blue Mountains last winter, one of which, an adult male specimen, was procured.   This species evinces a preference for the country lying between Normanton on the Gulf of Carpentaria, and Townsville on the North-eastern coast of Queensland, on the grassy plains of which they are occasionally captured and sent to the southern markets.   Like all the members of the *Ploceidæ* family it constructs a large dome shaped nest of dried grasses, which is usually placed in a low bush or tuft of long grass.   The eggs are five in number for a sitting, true ovals in form and pure white ; two specimens received from Dr. Henry Sinclair last season measure (A) 0·6 x 0·47 inch ; (B) 0·6 x 0·45 inch.

PTILOTIS FRENATA, *Ramsay.*   Bridled Honey-eater.

Ramsay, Proc. Zool. Soc., 1874, p. 603.

This species, one of the latest additions to the known *Meliphagidæ,* is found in the thickly timbered coastal ranges lying between Cairns and Cardwell in North-eastern Queensland.   A nest of this bird obtained by Mr. W. S. Day at Cairns on the 28th of November, 1891, and from which the parents were procured, was placed in a mass of creepers growing over a small shrub, at a height of about three feet from the ground ; it contained two eggs partially incubated.   The nest in question is built of stronger materials than is generally used by members of this genus, and was likewise unattached by the rim ; the eggs too are unlike those of typical specimens of the *Ptilotes,* approaching nearer in colour and disposition of their markings those of some members of the *Artamidæ.*   The nest is cup-shaped, and outwardly composed of long pliant stems of a climbing plant and portions of the soft reddish-brown stems of a small fern ; inside it is neatly lined with a white wiry looking vegetable fibre, forming a strong contrast to the reddish-brown hue of the exterior ; it measures 4·25 inches in diameter by 2·6 inches in height, internal diameter 2·5 inches x 1·6 inch in height.   The eggs are oval in form, tapering gently to the smaller end, and are white with minute dots and rounded markings of purplish-black and purplish-grey, the latter colour appearing as if beneath the surface of the shell, as usual the markings predominate on the thicker end where in places they become confluent and form an irregular zone ; with the exception of these zones, the markings on one of the specimens are larger and more sparingly dispersed, in the other they are uniformly distributed over the greater portion of the surface of the shell.   Length (A) 0·93 x 0·65 inch ; (B) 0·95 x 0·65 inch.

ORTHONYX SPINICAUDUS, *Temminck.*   Spine-tailed Orthonyx.

Gould, Handbk. Bds. Austr., Vol. i., sp. 372, p. 607.

The nest of the Spine-tailed Orthonyx is dome-shaped and large for the size of the bird, and resembles somewhat that of the Lyrebird, *M. superba*, but is much smaller and is usually placed between the buttresses of trees, or amongst the thick undergrowth in which this bird loves to dwell. A nest of this species now before me in the Group Collection of the Australian Museum, taken from the scrubs of the Richmond River in June 1890, (together with the parent birds and the eggs,) is domed in form, the base and sides of which are constructed of thick twigs about six inches in length, and the nest proper which has a lateral entrance, entirely of mosses, the whole structure with the exception of the opening being covered and well concealed with dead leaves ; it measures exteriorly from back to front of the base fourteen inches and a-half, width nine inches and a-half, height at the centre of the nest, seven inches, from front of the base to entrance of the nest proper, seven inches ; the interior of the nest which is rounded in form measures four inches in diameter. The eggs of this species are two in number for a sitting and are pure white and vary from an elongate oval to a compressed ellipse in form, the texture of the shell being fine and slightly glossy. Two sets measure as follows :—Length (A) 1·13 x 0·83 inch ; (B) 1·12 x 0·8 inch ; (C) 1·12 x 0·87 inch ; (D) 1·16 x 0·86 inch.

The coastal scrubs of New South Wales constitutes the principal habitat of this species.

CACOMANTIS INSPERATUS, *Gould.*   Square-tailed Brush-Cuckoo.
Gould, Handbk. Bds. Aust., Vol. i., sp. 380, p. 619.

Dr. George Hurst of Sydney, has taken at Newington on the Parramatta River, during many years past, eggs of a Cuckoo referable to this species, and which were usually obtained from the nests of *Rhipidura albiscapa:* and I have also seen similar eggs from the collections of Mr. John Waterhouse and Mr. Leslie Oakes taken in the same locality. A few years ago Dr. Hurst found one of the same Cuckoo's eggs at Newington in the nest of *Malurus cyaneus*, and to which he drew attention in the Proceedings of the Linnean Society of New South Wales, Vol. iii., 2nd Series, p. 421, 1888 ; attributing it to this species. Early in December 1891, Mr. S. Moore was successful in obtaining from a tree on the banks of the Cook's River a similar Cuckoo's egg from the nest of *Ptilotis chrysops*, and on the 26th of the same month in company with Dr. Hurst, two more Cuckoo's eggs were obtained at Eastwood, both from the nests of *Rhipidura albiscapa*, and which also contained the usual complement of eggs laid by this bird for a sitting. All these Cuckoo's eggs were obtained within a radius of ten miles of Sydney, and it is a matter of regret, that the opportunity was not taken of placing them in nests convenient for observation and hatching the young birds out, as was done by Dr. Ramsay and his brothers at Dobroyde, with the eggs of *C.*

pallidus, C. flabelliformis, L. plagosus, and *L. basalis,* so as to conclusively determine to which species they belong; but there can be no doubt Dr. Hurst was right in ascribing the eggs obtained by him and his friends to *Cuculus insperatus,* as it is the only other species of Cuckoo found near Sydney, the eggs of which we were until then unacquainted with. The eggs of this Cuckoo are not unlike large specimens of those of *Rhipidura albiscapa,* but the bluish-grey sub-surface markings predominate more than in those of the White-shafted Fantail ; they are a thick ovoid in form, of a creamy white ground colour, thickly spotted and blotched with yellowish-brown markings, intermingled with others of a dull bluish-grey, becoming larger on the thicker end of the egg, where they are confluent and form a well defined zone. Length (A) 0·72 x 0·53 inch ; (B) 0·7 x 0·58 inch ; (C) 0·73 x 0·58 inch ; (D) 0·73 x 0·56 inch ; (E) 0·7 x 0·53 inch.

With the exception of Northern Australia, this species is very sparingly dispersed over the remainder of the Continent in favourable situations.

CENTROPUS PHASIANUS, *Latham.* Swamp Pheasant.

Gould, Handbk. Bds. Austr., Vol. i., sp. 388, p. 634.

Mr. Charles Barnard, of Coomooboolaroo, Dawson River, Queensland, has kindly sent the following notes :—

"On the 15th of February, 1891, I found a nest and three eggs of *Centropus phasianus.* The nest was built about fifteen inches above the ground in some high broad-bladed grass, the tops of which were drawn down and loosely interwoven into the shape of a ball of about eight inches internal diameter, with a round hole in one side for entrance and another at the opposite side as a means of exit. The bottom of the nest was thickly padded with " Blood-wood*" leaves, which extended through the entrance and on to the bent down grass outside the nest in the shape of a platform. The nest was built against the stem of a small tree, I think for protection, as the grass all round appeared equally suitable for nesting in."

Mr. J. A. Boyd of the Herbert River, Queensland, informs me that a nest of this species was obtained on his plantation on the 16th of December, 1891, containing five eggs, and another on the 30th instant, with five young ones in it. In both instances these nests were constructed in the lower leaves of the Screw Palm, *(Pandanus aquaticus).*

Three of the above set of eggs are rounded in form, white, and nest-stained, the shell having a thin calcareous covering making the surface perfectly smooth, which is dull and lustreless ; in some places are scratches which appear to have been done by the parent bird while sitting, revealing the true character of the shell under-

---

* *Eucalyptus corymbosa.*

neath, they measure as follows :—length (A) 1·53 x 1·23 inch ;
(B) 1·39 x 1·17 inch ; (C) 1·48 x 1·2 inch.

Specimens of this bird similar to those of the Eastern coast
have been procured by Mr. E. H. Saunders at Roeburne, and the
late T. H. Boyer-Bower at Derby in North-western Australia,
it is also found at intervals throughout the coastal districts of
Northern and Eastern Australia, and although common in the
Northern portions of New South Wales, its range does not extend
so far south as the southern boundary of the colony.

CALYPTORHYNCHUS FUNEREUS, *Shaw.*   Funeral Black Cockatoo.
Gould, Hawlbk. Bds. Austr., Vol. ii., sp. 401, p. 20.

Unlike most members of the order Psittaci inhabiting Australia
which breed at the latter end of Spring and all through the Summer, the genus *Calyptorhynchus* does not commence to breed until
late in the Autumn or the beginning of Winter. In the previous
Supplement* it will be seen from Mr. E. H. Lane's notes, that
during a period of twelve years he had always obtained the
eggs of *C. solandri* during the months of March, April, and May,
and from the following notes sent at various times by Mr. George
Barnard of the Dawson River, Queensland it may be gathered
that *C. funereus* is an early Winter breeder.

"On the 2nd of June, 1884, my sons found a nest of *C. funereus*
containing two eggs. The nesting place was in the hollow bough
of a tall Eucalyptus." "June 9th, 1890—Yesterday my sons
found a nest of *C. funereus,* unfortunately the eggs were just
hatching, one was out, the other egg chipped : though we knew
they bred in June, we did not think they would be so early."

On the 13th June 1891, "my sons found two nests of *C.
funereus* and two of *C. solandri,* about ten miles from the homestead. Each nest contained but a single egg, all of which were
perfectly fresh, but as the holes in the trees had all been enlarged
by chopping and they were so far from home the eggs were taken.
All the nests were within a mile of each other and were in the
hollow boughs of lofty *Eucalypts; C. funereus* was from thirty to
forty feet from the ground, and deep down in the hollow trunk
of the tree, *C. solandri* were from seventy to ninety feet from the
ground, and the eggs could almost be reached from the hole."

"A fortnight after finding the nests of the Black Cockatoos
my sons went out again in the hopes that some of the birds would
have relaid. Only one nest was found to be occupied, that of *C.
funereus,* containing two eggs; which are rounder than those
taken previously.

The eggs of *C. funereus* vary somewhat in size and are rounded
in form, pure white, except where stained with the decaying wood

---

* Rec. Austr. Aus., Vol. i., No. 6, March 1891.

on which they were laid, the shell being dull and lustreless, and having minute shallow pittings all over them ; they measure (A) 1·82 x 1·49 inch ; (B) 1·9 x 1·6 inch.

The range of this species extends over Eastern and Southern Australia and Tasmania, although in the latter colony Gould separated the species from *C. funereus*, under the name of *C. xanthonotus*, but the specific characters are not constant, specimens having been received from Tasmania that could not be distinguished from the continental form, and Dr. Ramsay who has examined one of Gould's types, states they are identical.

POLYTELIS ALEXANDRÆ, *Gould.*   The Princess of Wales Parrakeet.

Gould, Handbk. Bds. Austr., Vol. ii., 1865, sp. 407, p. 32.

Much attention has recently been drawn to this the rarest of all the Australian Psittaci.   It was first discovered by Mr. F. G. Waterhouse at Howell's Ponds, in Lat. about 17° S. and Long. 133° E. who accompanied Stuart, the well known Central Australian explorer in 1862.   Gould described it in the following year in the Proceedings of the Zoological Society, dedicating it to the Princess of Wales, and subsequently figuring it in his Supplement to the Birds of Australia, in 1869.

After a lapse of twenty-eight years since discovering this species, Mr. M. Symonds Clark, of Adelaide, South Australia, brought under the notice of the public, through the columns of the *South Australian Register* of the 28th of August, 1890, the existence of two living specimens of *Polytelis alexandræ*, which had been taken from a nest in the hollow branch of a tree by Mr. T. G. Magarey at "Crown Point," about fifty miles north of "Charlotte Waters," in Lat. 25° 30′ and Long. 133°, about six hundred miles south from where the type specimens were obtained. Later on Dr. E. C. Stirling, the Director of the Adelaide Museum, who accompanied the Earl of Kintore, Governor of South Australia, on his trip across the Continent from north to south in 1891, succeeded in obtaining two specimens a few miles north of "Newcastle Waters," and towards the latter end of the same year Mr. A. H. C. Zietz, the Assistant Director of the Adelaide Museum, acquired the eggs of this species, one of which together with a male specimen of *P. alexandræ*, has recently been received by the Trustees of the Australian Museum.

The egg of *P. alexandræ* is an ellipse in form, pure white, the texture of the shell being very fine, and the surface slightly glossy.   Length 1·23 inch x 0·94 inch in breadth.

The interior of Northern Central Australia constitutes the habitat of this species.

TURNIX MELANOTUS, *Gould.*   Small Black-spotted Turnix.

Gould, Handbk. Bds. Austr., Vol. ii., sp. 481, p. 182.

*Of the three small species of *Turnix* found in Australia, two of them, *T. velox* and *T. pyrrhothorax*, give decided preference to the open grassy plains of the inland districts, while *Turnix melanotus* is essentially an inhabitant of the low marshy ground and damp scrubs contiguous to the eastern coast of Australia. Near Sydney the latter species is not uncommon in the neighbourhood of Randwick, Botany, and La Perouse, localities also frequented by the Least Swamp Quail, *Excalfatoria australis*, and both species, shot at Botany on the same day, have been recently presented to the Museum.

The nidification of *Turnix melanotus*, similar to that of other members of the genus, is a scantily grass-lined hollow in the ground, sheltered by a convenient tuft of grass or low bush. The eggs are four in number for a sitting; specimens obtained on Mr. Boyd's plantation on the Herbert River, Queensland, on the 13th of December, 1890, are oval in form, tapering somewhat sharply to the smaller end, the ground colour is of a greyish-white, and is almost obscured with minute freckles of pale umber-brown, while sparingly distributed over the surface of the shell are conspicuous spots and blotches of dark slaty-grey, which in some places approach an inky-black hue. Length (A) 0·97 x 0·73 inch, (B) 0·98 x 0·73 inch. These eggs can easily be distinguished from those of *T. velox*, by being much darker and the surface of the shell bright and glossy. During the same month, eggs of *Excalfatoria australis* were procured in the same locality. The latter species, Mr. J. A. Boyd informs me, is very common on the Herbert River.

STERNA MEDIA, *Horsfield.*   Crested Tern.

Sterna media, Horsfield, Trans. Linn. Soc., 1820, xiii., p. 198.
Sterna bengalensis, Lesson, Traite d'Orn., p. 621 (1831); Gould,
     Handbk. Bds. Austr., Vol. ii., p. 327, sp. 603 (1865).
Thalasseus torresii, Gould, Proc. Zool. Soc., (1842), p. 142; *id.*
     Bds. Austr., fol. Vol. vii. pl. 25.

This species of Tern has a most extensive range of habitat. It is found frequenting the Northern and Eastern coast of Africa, the Red Sea, and the southern shores of Asia, the Indo-Malayan and Austro-Malayan Archipelago, and the Northern and Eastern coasts of Australia.

Mr. H. Greusill Barnard, who has lately returned from a collecting tour in the islands contiguous to the coast of North-eastern Queensland, has kindly sent the following interesting

---

* North, Rec. Austr. Mus., Vol. i., No. 9, October, 1891.

notes respecting the nidification of this Tern, also several of its eggs for description, and a skin of one of the parent birds for identification.

"In conversation with the keeper of a fishing station on a small island, about six miles south of North Barnard Island, I learnt that a species of Tern was breeding in great numbers, on a small sand-bank thirty miles due east of the latter island and close to the Great Barrier Reef. One of the fishing boats coming in on Saturday night, I took my gun and went on board; sail was set soon after, but I did not reach the scene of operations till Monday morning, the 23rd of November, 1891. The bank was a very small one not more than twenty yards across, and about three or four feet above high water in the centre. On approaching it we could see the Terns sitting on the sand in hundreds, also several of a very much larger species of sea-bird*, which I ascertained afterwards on landing were engaged in eating the eggs of the Terns, as I found a great number of the eggs with a large hole pecked in the side. The eggs of the Terns were placed on the bare sand, one to each bird for a sitting, and so close together as only to give the birds room to sit; there could have been no less than five or six hundred eggs on that portion of the bank occupied. Though the birds had been breeding more than a month, there were no young ones, the fishermen informing me that the larger species we saw on the bank devoured the young ones directly they were hatched. I shot two of the parent-birds, and the men collected about two buckets full of eggs to cook."

The eggs are oval in form, some of which are sharply pointed at the smaller end and vary in ground colour from a delicate reddish-white to stone and lustreless white, some specimens are boldly blotched and spotted with penumbral markings of purplish and reddish-brown, and underlying blotches and spots of bluish and pearl-grey appearing as if beneath the surface of the shell; others are uniformly dotted and spotted with smaller markings of the same colours, but in all the specimens now before me the markings on the outer surface of the shell are mostly penumbral. Average specimens measure, length (A) 2·02 x 1·47 inch; (B) 2·1 x 1·4 inch; (C) 2·05 x 1·43 inch; (D) 2·08 x 1·42 inch.

PLOTUS NOVÆ-HOLLANDIÆ, *Gould.* The New Holland Snake-bird or Darter.

Gould, Handbk. Bds. Austr., Vol. ii., sp. 657, p. 496.

†The Trustees of the Australian Museum have lately received the eggs of *Plotus novæ-hollandiæ,* taken by Mr. J. L. Ayres at

---

* Probably a Skua.
† North, Rec. Austr. Mus., Vol. i., No. 7, June, 1891.

Lake Buloke, in the Wimmera District of Victoria, on 1st April, 1891. The nest was built at a height of about fifteen feet, on the branch of a Eucalyptus standing in the water, it was outwardly composed of sticks lined inside with twigs, and contained five eggs, one of which was unfortunately broken in descending the tree. The eggs are elongated ovals in form tapering gradually towards the smaller end, where they are somewhat sharply pointed; the shell has a thick, white, calcareous covering, only a few scratches here and there revealing the true colour underneath, which is of a pale blue. Length (A) 2·41 x 1·45 inches ; (B) 2·32 x 1·42 inches ; (C) 2·34 x 1·45 inch ; (D) 2·43 x 1·47 inch. Although very late in the season, Mr. Ayres found another Darter's nest on the same day, containing five newly hatched young ones.

This species is found all over Australia, but is more sparingly distributed in the extreme Southern and Western portions of the Continent.

NOTE ON THE OCCURRENCE OF THE SANDERLING (CALIDRIS ARENARIA) IN NEW SOUTH WALES.

By Prof. ALFRED NEWTON, M.A., F.R.S.

HAVING lately occasion to investigate the range of the Sanderling (Calidris arenaria), I came across a memorandum made in the year 1860 of my having then seen in the Derby Museum at Liverpool, two specimens of the larger race of this species, one in Winter dress and the other in incipient Spring plumage, both being marked as females and as having been obtained at Sandy Cove in New South Wales, 20th April, 1844, by the late John Macgillivray. As this wandering species does not seem to have been hitherto recorded from Australia, this fact may be of some interest to the Ornithologists of that country. I may add that I find little verification of Temminck's assertion in 1840 (Man. d' Ornithologie iv. p. 349) often repeated in one form or another that the Sanderling occurs in the Sunda Islands and New Guinea; or even, as by a recent writer who states in general terms, that it is a winter visitor to the islands of the Malay Archipelago ("Geographical Distribution of the Charadriidæ &c." p. 432). Java seems to be the only one of these islands in which its presence has been determined, and though it was included with a mark of doubt in the lists of the Birds of Borneo by Prof. W. Blasius (1882) and Dr. Vorderman (1886) respectively, it has been omitted, and apparently with reason from that of Mr. Everitt (1889). It is well known to pass along the whole of the West Coast of America, and it has been obtained in the Galapagos and the Sandwich Islands, but I know of no instance of its having been observed in any polynesian group or within the tropics to the eastward of Java.

Magdalene College, Cambridge, 25th March, 1892.

ON SOME UNDESCRIBED REPTILES AND FISHES FROM AUSTRALIA.

By J. DOUGLAS OGILBY.

TYPHLOPS CURTUS, *sp. nov.*

Habit stout. Snout obtusely rounded, and moderately prominent; nostrils inferior. Rostral narrow, its upper portion three and two-thirds in the width of the head, extending to between the anterior margins of the eyes; nasal incompletely divided, the cleft originating above the first labial, forming a suture with the prefrontal; preocular smaller than the ocular. Eye distinct. Prefrontal very large, much larger than the supraoculars; frontal and parietals not larger than the body-scales. Four upper labials. Diameter of body twenty-four times in the total length. Tail longer than broad, ending in a strong, short, conical spine, which scarcely projects beyond the surrounding scales. Twenty-three series of scales round the middle of the body, the dorsals and laterals smooth, the abdominals conspicuously raised along the median line, with numerous faint carinations on the basal half, and with the tips free.

Colors.—Pale reddish-brown above, each scale broadly margined with gray; head-shields darker, chestnut-brown with a yellow margin; lower surfaces yellow.

Dimensions.

Total length	...	...	...	275 mm.
Head	...	...	...	7 ,,
Width of head	...	...	...	7 ,,
Body	...	...	...	259 ,,
Tail	...	...	...	9 ,,
Breadth of tail	...	...	...	8 ,,

Habitat.—Walsh River, Gulf of Carpentaria.

Type.—In the Australian Museum, presented by E. G. Braddon, Esq. Reg. No. R. 1132.

HOPLOCEPHALUS SUBOCCIPITALIS, *sp. nov.*

Body moderate. Head depressed, rather small. Eye of moderate size, its diameter rather more than half the length of the snout, with rounded pupil; supraciliary ridge but little developed. The height of the rostral is three-fourths of its breadth, its upper margin rounded, just visible from above; length of the frontonasals five-sevenths of that of the prefrontals, which are half that of the frontal ; the latter shield hexagonal, obtusely angular anteriorly, acutely so posteriorly, the lateral margins slightly converging, one-half longer than broad ; length of the parietals equal to that of the frontals and prefrontals together ; the nasal forms a short suture with the preocular ; two subequal postoculars ; six upper labials, the third and fourth entering the eye, the first small, the others gradually increasing in size to the last ; two pairs of temporals, the lower one of the anterior pair much the largest, and partially wedged in between the two last labials. There are 17 scales round the middle of the body ; abdominal shields 163 ; two anal plates, with sometimes a third smaller plate in front ; subcaudal shields in a single series, 43 in number.

Colors.—Head above olive-brown, with a broad black band including the greater portion of the parietals and two series of scales behind them, and bending angularly forwards upon the posterior third of the frontal, and extending down the sides of the head to behind the last upper labial ; dorsal and lateral scales bright olive-brown, the latter tipped with black ; abdominal and subcaudal scales pale yellow ; the former with a roseate spot on the median series and a dusky spot on the postero-external angles ; the latter with faint indications of dark median spots.

Dimensions.

Total length	...	...	...	370 mm.
Head	...	...	...	12 ,,
Width of head	...	...	...	7 ,,
Body	...	...	...	300 ,,
Tail	...	...	...	58 ,,

Habitat.—Moree.

Type.—In the Australian Museum, presented by E. J. Ross McMaster, Esq.   Reg. No. R. 1127.

CLUPEA SPRATTELLIDES, *sp. nov.*

D. 15.   A. 19.   V. 8.   P. 16.   C. 19.   L. lat. 49 – 51.   L. tr. 12 – 13.   Vert. 48.

Length of head 5·00 – 5·15, of caudal fin 5·75 – 6·00, height of body 4·75 – 5·00 in the total length. Eye moderate, with rudimentary adipose lid, its diameter 3·00 - 3·20 in the length of the head ; snout short and obtuse, 1·10 – 1·25 in the diameter of the eye ; interorbital space slightly convex, 1·40 – 1·55 in the same. Nostrils small and approximate, situated midway between the tip of the snout and the orbit, the posterior the larger, subcircular. Upper surface of the head flat, with a strong central ridge from the snout to the occiput, which is depressed : lower jaw projecting : cleft of mouth small and very oblique, the maxilla reaching to beneath the anterior third of the orbit. Opercles smooth ; subopercle moderately broad, acutely rounded behind. Toothless. The distance between the origin of the dorsal and the tip of the snout is equal to or a trifle longer than that between the same point and the base of the caudal ; the third ray is the longest, from 1·50 - 1·66 in the length of the head, and equal to the basal length of the fin ; the outer margin is concave : anal low, the longest rays a little more than the diameter of the eye : *ventrals inserted entirely in front of the dorsal*, with the outer margin acutely rounded, their length from 2·00 – 2·15 in that of the head ; pectorals rounded, their length 1·50 – 1·60 in the same ; the upper basal angle vertically beneath the posterior margin of the opercle : caudal forked, the least height of the pedicle 2·25 – 2·40 in the height of the body. Scales moderate, feebly carinated, and firmly adherent ; a patch of small scales on each side of the occipital depression ; no triangular scale above the origin of the ventrals : a series of scutes similar to those on the abdominal profile between the occiput and the dorsal ; behind that fin the profile of the back is smooth and rounded : abdominal scutes well developed, twenty in front and twelve to fourteen behind the origin of the ventrals. Gill-rakers moderately stout and closely set, their length about one-third of the diameter of the eye.

Colors.—Pale straw with a broad silvery median band ; each scale above the lateral band with a crescentic series of black dots near the posterior margin ; snout similiarly dotted. Fins hyaline.

Type.—In the Australian Museum. Reg. No. I. 3034.

The species above described inhabits the rivers flowing into Port Jackson and Botany Bay ; it has been known to the writer for some time, but as has probably been the case with previous investigators of our Fish-fauna, it was set aside without examination, under the belief that it was merely the young of the widely distributed *C. nova-hollandiæ* : having, however, had occasion of late to examine more closely our New South Wales Clupeids, the present species attracted a more careful investigation with the gratifying result given above.

C. sprattellides is occasionally brought to market in considerable numbers among the prawns *(Penæus mackayi)* from the Parramatta, George's, and Cook's Rivers.

The type specimens described above measure from two and two-thirds to three and a half inches, the latter being apparently the full size to which the species attains. No signs of spawning could be observed in the example dissected.

The position of the ventral fins in *C. sprattellides* being apparently anomalous in the genus *Clupea*, and the fact that this character is associated with a well developed dorsal scutation forces upon us the consideration whether these characters, taken separately or in conjunction, should not entitle this and similar forms to generic rank. The latter character, however, that is the acute spiniferous ridge between the occiput and the dorsal fin, is common to all the fresh-water and estuary non-migratory Herrings of the cismontane rivers of the Colony, between the limits of the Richmond River and Botany Bay, which the author has had an opportunity of examining : the former character, that of the position of the ventral fin, has been extensively used by systematists as one on which to base a separate genus. This is not the place to discuss the importance or otherwise of this character, but it is worthy of notice that in our common fresh-water herring (*Clupea novæ-hollandiæ*, Cuv. & Val. = *C. richmondia*, Macl. = (?) *C. vittata*, Casteln.) the ventral fins are inserted immediately below the origin of the dorsal.

With regard to the dorsal serrature, we appeal to our fellow-workers in other countries to examine more carefully the anadromous herrings of their rivers and estuaries, for should it prove to be the case that all the fresh-water herrings have this characteristic, they are clearly separable from the typical *Clupea*.

All species, therefore, in which the occipito-dorsal serrature is present, might be separated therefrom under the name of *Hyperlophus*, and distinguished from *Clupea* by this character.

ON THE STRUCTURE AND AFFINITIES OF *PANDA ATOMATA*, Gray.*

By C. HEDLEY, F.L.S.

[Plates IV. V. VI.]

SOME uncertainty appears to prevail regarding the position which *Bulimus atomatus*, Gray, should occupy. The latest volume of the "Monographia Heliceorum Viventium" includes it in a section embracing another Australian and a dozen South American species, an arrangement which must surely violate natural

*Since this essay was written I learn that, by an old coincidence, both Mr. Pilsbry and myself independently arrived at the conclusion that *atomata* should correctly be referred to *Panda*, and published our opinions simultaneously in America and Australia, in "The Nautilus," Vol. VI., No. 1, p. 9, May, 1892; and in the "Abstract" of the Proceedings of the Linn. Soc. N.S.W., April, 1892, respectively.

affinities. Albers' classification, "Die Heliceen," p. 229, though more correct, is not in accordance with the views of the writer, who has recently enjoyed an opportunity of studying this interesting creature alive in the recesses of its native forests. The following is the first record of the soft parts of this snail. The animal so resembles the figure of *Caryodes dufresni* appearing in the *P.L.S., N.S.W.* (2) vi. Pl. iii. f. 1. that this sketch would almost as well represent the former as the latter species. Colour ; a pale ochreous yellow becoming redder on the head and tentacles ; a dark brownish-black dorsal stripe extends from between the tentacles to the mantle, a similar but fainter stripe extends on either side along the facial groove from the lips to the mantle ; sole of foot ashy-blue ; mantle ashy-blue shot with ochreous yellow. Some snails are paler and some darker than the one described. Total length 70 mm., muzzle projecting 25 mm. in front, tail projecting 7 mm. behind the shell when crawling ; tentacles 15 mm. long, bases 5 mm. apart ; measured just in advance of the shell, the body is 15 mm. wide and 12 mm. high. Tentacles gradually tapering to one-third of the diameter of their bases, clad with fine longitudinal granulations ; ocular bulbs asymmetrical, more swollen on the lower distal side, eye superior central in position. Two ill-defined grooves start from the mantle and enclose a series of rugæ which compose the dark median dorsal colour-band mentioned above ; anteriorly these grooves are lost in the reticulations around the bases of the tentacles. From the median line, reticulating grooves extending outwards and downwards, intersect a series of prominent long narrow tubercles, from six to ten of which intervene between the dorsal band and the facial groove. The tail is rather flat and sharply pointed ; the sides and tail are covered by flat, irregular polygonal tubercles which become smaller on approaching the tail. On emerging from its shell, *atomata* has a habit of spreading the margin of the foot into a wide, flat flange. I note that the left side of the mantle developes no rudimentary mantle lobes as in *Hadra*. When extended, the shell is carried slightly obliquely, the apex being a little to the right of the tail ; when retracted, the animal does not usually shrink further back than the aperture, to which no epiphragm was observed.

The living snails were collected by Dr. Cox and the writer in tolerable abundance in a "cedar-brush" adjoining Mr. Ashford's estate on Sparke's Creek, near Scone, N.S.W. Their habit was to nestle beneath decaying logs or in drifts of fallen leaves, where they would occur singly or by twos and threes ; one was taken in the act of ascending a tree a few feet from the ground. Specimens were obtained (April 1892) in all stages of growth. Dr. Cox informs me that on other occasions he has found this species to lay large, white, hard-shelled eggs.

The reproductive system of this form seems to me to be especially worthy of attention. Branching from the vagina, opposite to the entrance of the duct of the spermatheca, is a gland of unknown function, marked X in the accompanying illustration (Pl. v. fig. 13); this exactly corresponds to the gland marked x in Semper's illustrations of the genitalia of *falconeri* and *dufresni*, and also to the gland marked v. p. in the figure of the genitalia of *cunninghami* published by the author. It will be observed that Semper's drawings show a short, wide, recurved duct, and mine a narrow, subcylindrical one. On referring to a sketch of the organs of *dufresni*, which I took some time ago, I notice that the gland in question appears of the form observed in *cunninghami* and *atomata*; possibly each form may be proper to different periods of gestation. No other Australian helices are known to possess such an appendage, and its value as a means of classification cannot be denied. The musculature, which is shared by the species with which I would associate *atomata*, is also peculiar. The retractor muscle of the penis is not attached to the floor of the pulmonary cavity as in some helices, but is a broad band arising from the main retractor muscle of the columella. The narrow subcylindrical portion of the penis sheath extending from the insertion of the retractor muscle to the origin of the vas deferens, is also strictly analogous to the similar portions of *cunninghami, falconeri* and *dufresni*. The ovo-testis is a compact, yellow, bi-lobed body, not ramifying through the lobes of the liver.

The jaw (Pl. v, fig. 11) is 4½ mm. long, smooth, boomerang-shaped, ends tapering to a blunt point, cutting margin with a slight median projection.

The radula (Pl. vi. figs. 14, 15) measures 10 x 3 mm., is strap-shaped, formula, 185 rows of 45 : 22 : 1 : 22 : 45.; the rachidian is single, narrow, about the length of its base, sagittate at the root, slender in the stem, lanceolate at the apex, basal plate expanded posteriorly; laterals more bulky than the rachidian, unicuspidate, broadly ovate, apex acute, projecting past the basal margin, alate angle slightly expanded; the remoter laterals pass gradually into the marginals, which are characterised by single, entire, oval, much inclined cusps.

The classification of this species hitherto accepted seeming to the writer in disaccord with its real relationships, he would prefer to intercalate it among other Australian snails as follows :—

Family HELICIDÆ.

Foot flat, pointed, without mucous gland or pedal line; mantle without appendages; tentacles long and tapering.

Group MACROÖN.

Egg large, hard-shelled; apex of shell consisting of 2-2½ whorls of embryonic shell, sharply marked off and differently sculptured from the adult.

A.—Genital system furnished with an additional gland.   Jaw oxygnathous.

    Panda falconeri, Reeve.
       ,,   ,,   var. maconelli, Reeve.
       ,,   ,,   ,, azonata, Hedley.
       ,,   ,,   ,, tigris, Hedley.
       ,,   atomata, Gray.
       ,,   ,,   var. kershawi, Brazier.
       ,,   ,,   ,, elongata, Hedley.
       ,,   ,,   ,, azonata, Hedley.
       ,,   larreyi, Brazier.
    Pedinogyra cunninghami, Gray.
       ,,   ,,   var. mühlfeldtiana, Pfeiffer.
       ,,   ,,   ,, compressa, Mousson.
       ,,   ,,   ,, minor, Mousson.
    Caryodes dufresni, Leach.

B.—Without the additional gland.

Ba.—Jaw oxygnathous; lateral teeth of radula simple.
    Anoglypta launcestonensis, Reeve.

*Bb.—Jaw goniognathous; lateral teeth of radula with accessory cusp.

    Liparus inflatus, Lamarck.
       ,,   ,,   var. melo, Quoy & G.
       ,,   ,,   ,, physodes, Menke.
       ,,   ,,   ,, castaneus, Pfeiffer.
       ,,   ,,   ,, bulla, Menke.
       ,,   ,,   ,, rhodostoma, Gray.
       ,,   baconi, Benson.
       ,,   tasmanicus, Pfeiffer.
       ,,   mastersi, Cox.
       ,,   kingi, Gray.
       ,,   ,, var. trilineatus, Quoy & G.
       ,,   angasianus, Pfeiffer.
       ,,   brazieri, Angas.
       ,,   onslowi, Cox.
       ,,   dux, Pfeiffer.

The anatomical information on which the above synopsis is based chiefly consists of these illustrations and their accompany ing letterpress:—Reis. im. Phil. III., Pl. xii. fig. 20, genitalia of

---

*Polynesian representatives of *Liparus* would appear to be *Placostylus*, and its derivatives *Diplomorpha* and *Partula*.

falconeri : figs. 23, 24, 25, ditto *dufresni ;* Pl. xv. fig. 14, ditto *melo ;* Pl. xvi. fig. 7, radula of *dufresni ;* fig. 10, ditto *falconeri ;* Pl. xvii. fig. 13, ditto *melo ;* Proc. Roy. Soc. Queensland, VI., Pl. iii. jaw, radula and genitalia of *cunninghami :* Pl. xiv. jaw and radula of *mastersi ;* P.L.S., N.S.W. (1) III. Pl. vii. fig. 1*a*, egg of *dufresni :* op. cit. (2) VI. Pl. ii. fig. 1, jaw of *dufresni ;* figs. 2, 3 and 4, jaw, radula and genitalia of *tasmanicus ;* figs. 5, 6 and 7, jaw, radula and genitalia of *launcestonensis.*

Should a lens be applied to the summit of a fresh specimen of any of the species enumerated above, the apex (Pl. v. fig. 10) will be seen to resemble a well worn thimble ; the first two whorls are usually dome-shaped, and are always marked off from the adult shell by an oblique furrow. *Anoglypta* may perhaps be regarded as most retaining the ancestral sculpture. A wide band or bands round the base or periphery is a colour-pattern that is apt to occur throughout the group. The bands so conspicuous in *dufresni* recur in *inflatus* var. *castaneus*, in *bucovi*, and in *augasianus ;* they are represented on the base of *Anoglypta*, can be traced in the wide bands around the base of *falconeri*, and the pattern is distinctly repeated in some colour varieties of *cunninghami.* Another feature in common is the bluish-gleaming sub-nacreous lining of the interior of the shell.

Allusion is made above to the egg of *atomata.* Tenison-Woods figured the egg of *C. dufresni*, and it was re-described by the writer, P.L.S., N.S.W. (2) VI. p. 20. *A. launcestonensis* is reported (op. cit. p. 22) to lay a similar egg. A broken egg of *cunninghami*, collected by Mr. S. Stutchbury, is now in the Australian Museum, and is figured Pl. v. fig 12. It may be described as globose, 9 mm. in diameter, hard, calcareous, brittle, white, coarsely granular without, smooth within.

The subordination, in the foregoing synopsis, of *maconelli* to *falconeri* as a variety, is an innovation that demands an explanation which Plate iv. is intended to convey. In the latest notice of the genus, Pilsbry succinctly sums up the difference by stating (Man. Conch., 2nd Ser., Vol VI. p. 76) that *maconelli* is "Just like *H. falconeri* in color and sculpture, but narrower and and imperforate." It is here contended that a large series admits of a perfect graduation, traceable from the tightly coiled, narrow, elevated and imperforate *maconelli*, to the looser coiled, wide, depressed and umbilicate *falconeri ;* while extreme forms exist more elevated and more depressed than either of Reeve's illustrations. Reduced outlines of Reeve's types of *maconelli* and *falconeri* are represented by figs. 1 and 6 respectively ; figs. 2 and 8 are the extremes of each form as figured in the Monograph of Australian Land Shells ; figs. 3, 4 and 5 are original sketches, from examples selected and lent for the purpose by Dr. Cox, to show the transition from *maconelli* to *falconeri ;* while fig. 7 is another original sketch, from a shell in the Australian Museum, intermediate between Cox's and Reeve's conception of *falconeri*. Did space suffice, and necessity demand, a further series of intermediate forms might be furnished more closely linking the one to the other of the preceding instances; but enough are afforded, it is supposed, to prove "quod erat demonstrandum."

Panda thus gives a curious and instructive illustration of the value placed by the elder systematists upon "Bulimus" and "Helix," since Reeve assigned *maconelli* to the former and *falconeri* to the latter, an arrangement in which Pfeiffer quite acquiesced. Two colour varieties of this species might with advantage be distinguished.

VAR. AZONATA, var. nov.

Bandless, entire shell straw-yellow coloured.

VAR. TIGRIS, var. nov.

The original dark spiral bands have here become disintegrated into separate blotches, and these latter have further become confluent with those above and beneath, so that the band pattern is changed from regularly spiral to irregularly longitudinal and zigzag, in which state it approaches the pattern of *atomata* and *larreyi*.

In this genus, neither contour nor colouration can be relied upon to furnish specific characters, and I cannot admit *kershawi*, Brazier (P.Z.S., 1871, p 641) as a valid species. No habitat has been recorded for this form between the valleys of the Hunter and of the Snowy River. Yet, despite their geographical isolation, southern specimens can be precisely matched, as Dr. Cox has kindly demonstrated to me, by northern shells. Fossil specimens of this species have been identified by Dr. Cox from Victoria, but none have come under the writer's observation, nor is he aware of any mention of the fact in the literature of the subject.

I add a sketch of the as yet unfigured *kershawi*, from the author's type, now in the collection of the Australian Museum.

Other variations of this species are—

VAR. ELONGATA, var. nov.

More elevated than the type, and represented by Mon. Austr. L. Shells, Pl. xviii., fig. 15.

VAR. AZONATA, var. nov.

Bandless, entire shell straw-yellow coloured.

NOTE ON THE

NIDIFICATION of *MANUCODIA COMRII*, Sclater.

Comrie's Manucode.

By A. J. NORTH, F.L.S., Assistant in Ornithology.

[Plate VII.]

Manucodia comrii, Sclat., Proc. Zool. Soc., 1876, p. 459.

The Trustees of the Australian Museum have lately received from the Rev. R. H. Rickard the egg of *Manucodia comrii*, taken by him on Fergusson Island, off the South-East coast of New Guinea, in July, 1891. The Rev. Mr. Rickard informs me that from the 20th of June to the 20th of July he had been at various times engaged in company with his black boy shooting Manucodes on this island, but rarely saw a female. Early in July he found a nest of this species in the lower branches of a bread-fruit tree at a height of twenty-five feet from the ground. The female was on the nest, which was an open loosely made structure of vinelets and twigs placed at the extremity of the branch; having procured her, he found that she was in very indifferent plumage as though she had been sitting for a long time, and the eggs, two in number, were chipped, and just upon the point of hatching. The egg is an elongate ovoid in form, and is of a warm isabelline ground colour with purplish dots, blotches and bold longitudinal streaks, uniformally dispersed over the surface of the shell, intermingled with similar superimposed markings of purplish-grey. Length 1·65 x 1·13 inch.

The range of this species is confined to the islands of the D'Entrecasteaux Group.

NOTE on SOME BISMUTH MINERALS, MOLYBDENITE, and ENHYDROS.

By A. Liversidge, M.A., F.R.S., Prof. of Chemistry, University of Sydney.

[Plates VIII. IX. X.]

The minerals mentioned in the following short note form part of a collection recently purchased by the Trustees of the Australian Museum; some of them are of unusual interest, hence it was considered desirable to draw attention to them in the pages of the "Museum Records." The numerals simply indicate the different specimens examined and described, those which are of the ordinary character and from well known localities are not mentioned in this paper.

Native Bismuth.

1. Some of the bismuth is in the massive condition, and is similar to specimens already described in the "Journal of the Royal Society of New South Wales," 1891, other specimens show it in the form of acicular crystals running through rock crystal. The massive bismuth is associated with quartz, both crystallised and massive, sulphide of bismuth, bismuth ochre, galena, the latter argentiferous, iron pyrites passing into ferrous sulphate, wolfram, molybdenite and tin stone. From Kingsgate, Glen Innes, N.S.W.

2. The acicular crystals in one case are two to three inches long and of about the thickness of a horse hair, these completely penetrate the rock crystal in much the same way as we often see acicular fibres of rutile; the characteristic colour, metallic lustre and cleavage of the metal being, however, well shown. This appears to be an unusual mode of occurrence for bismuth. Kingsgate.

3. Accompanying the fibres of the metal are small scattered crystals or specks of the metal, together with small columnar crystals. Kingsgate.

4. Native bismuth in quartz from Tingha, N.S.W.

5. Native bismuth, from Kangaroo Hills, Queensland. Associated with chlorite, quartz, and red oxide of iron or gossan.

6. Native bismuth, from Biggenden, Queensland. In calcite, where it occurs mainly between the cleavage planes of the calcite, which is strongly striated like some of the Scandinavian specimens of that mineral.

7. Native bismuth, in hornblende and quartz; Mt. Ramsay, Tasmania.

BISMUTH SULPHIDE.

1. In plates or films with a finely fibrous structure, embedded in rock crystal. The sulphide also occurs in granite made up of a brownish felspar, quartz and decomposed mica. From Kingsgate, Glen Innes, N.S.W.

2. Massive bismuth sulphide also possessing a fibrous structure, with the native metal, from the same place.

3. With bismuth carbonate and magnetite, Biggenden, Queensland.

BISMUTH CARBONATE.

1. This is of an ochrey form, associated with bismuth sulphide, quartz, etc. From Kingsgate, Glen Innes, N.S.W.

2. This specimen is massive, and possesses a platy or laminated structure.

3. Gold with bismuth carbonate, Yarrow Creek, N.S.W.

4. In a fourth specimen, from Biggenden, Queensland, the carbonate occurs with native bismuth in quartz, and is of a greyish colour, instead of the yellowish tint exhibited by the Kingsgate carbonate.

5. This specimen, from Mt. Shamrock, Queensland, is said to be auriferous.

6. From Halifax Bay, Queensland.

MOLYBDENITE (MoS_2).

[Plate viii.]

Found associated with native bismuth and other minerals, as already mentioned, in quartz. Some of the crystals have been found of very large size, as much as $3\frac{1}{2}$ x $5\frac{1}{2}$ inches, and built up to a thickness of 2 or 3 inches (Journ. Roy. Soc. N.S.W., p. 237, 1892); the outlines of such, however, are very imperfect, but amongst those in the present collection are some very well developed crystals (see plate viii. which shows the natural size), but of smaller size. The group (fig. 5) is a very interesting one, showing well marked hexagonal forms, with a nearly vertical crystal rising from, and crossing the horizontal ones. In other cases the plates of molybdenite penetrate the crystals of quartz, and pass between the adjacent faces of the rock crystal. Some of the quartz crystals are cavernous, and have the vugs lined with small crystals of quartz, showing the usual combination of the prism and pyramid. In one specimen the molybdenite is seated on tinstone. From Kingsgate, Glen Innes, N.S.W.

MOLYBDENUM OCHRE.

In the form of yellow patches consisting of felted acicular crystals. From Kingsgate, Glen Innes, N.S.W.

ENHYDROS, OR WATER STONES.

(Plates ix. x.)

No locality is given for these, but they so closely resemble those formerly found at Spring Creek, Beechworth, Victoria, that they in all probability come from that place. The specimens figured on plates ix. and x. are remarkable for their large size, the plates show them of their natural dimensions, except that plate x. is much foreshortened from a to b, being $7\frac{1}{2}$ inches in length instead of about $2\frac{5}{8}$ as shown. Plate ix. shows the hollow nature of these enhydros, where the ends having been broken off, the interior is thickly coated or lined with small pyramids of quartz crystals, the thicker one (plate x.) is also hollow, and each of the plates of which it is made up is likewise hollow or shows a tendency to form a cavity at the thicker parts; in some this is merely indicated by a crystalline structure. One of the enhydros, not figured, is attached to a lump of ordinary quartz. The outer surfaces of all of them are of very hard, smooth chalcedony, having a horny appearance and brownish colour, stained with iron oxide. The sp. gr. is 2·66, i.e. the usual sp. gr. of quartz. Hardness = 7·5. None of these three retained any liquid.

Mr. E. J. Dunn described the mode in which the enhydros occur at Spring Creek, in a paper read before the Royal Society of Victoria (Trans. R.S. of Vic., 1870, p. 32); they are found in a dyke in granite, the dyke is composed of fragments of granite and occasional pieces of sandstone cemented by crystallised quartz, together with large masses of coarse chalcedony and straight veins of chalcedony scales and clay. Mr. Dunn mentions that the enhydros vary in size from that of a split pea to five inches across, and that many of them contain a fluid; after a few days exposure they usually show an air bubble, in many the fluid disappears altogether in a few days; the walls of some are as thin as a sheet of paper and very fragile, while others have walls $\frac{1}{4}$ inch thick. On p. 71 of the same volume is a paper upon them by Mr. G. Foord, describing the enhydros more in detail, and giving an account of the contained fluid, which he describes as a dilute solution in water of chlorides and sulphates of sodium, magnesium and calcium, together with silicic acid.

Some smaller specimens in my possession have a much more regular geometrical form than the three under examination and belonging to the Museum. At first sight they might be mistaken for crystals, so smooth and regular are their faces, but a very little examination shows that this is not the case, practically none of the faces are parallel, and their forms do not correspond to any crystallographic system. I am inclined to think that they have been deposited within cracks and cavities formed in the clay (in which they are found), these cavities are probably due to the movements of the clay, parts having slid upon one another in the process of settlement, and a breccia-like structure set up with intermediate gaps and cavities. Mr. Foord's explanation that the chalcedony and quartz crystals have been deposited upon the walls of the cavities until the entrances to the hollow spaces were filled up (a portion of the liquid being thereby imprisoned) appears to satisfy the requirements of the case.

ADDITIONS to the AVIFAUNAS of TASMANIA, and NORFOLK and LORD HOWE ISLANDS.

By ALFRED J. NORTH, F.L.S., Assistant in Ornithology.

DURING the last twelve months an unusually large number of rare or additional grallatorial and natatorial species have been obtained in these insular areas. It is my intention here to briefly note the latter. Why one season should be better than another for aquatic nomads or visitors to make their appearance almost simultaneously in places so widely separated as Lord Howe Island, Norfolk Island, and Santo in the New Hebrides is probably due to exceptionally fine weather and favourable climatic adventitious aids conducive to long and extended flight, and not, as frequently occurs with arboreal species driven to seek a place of refuge, through tempestuous weather.

To begin with Tasmania, Dr. L. Holden of Circular Head, informs me that at the latter end of April of this year, he shot in that locality a fine adult male Blue-billed Duck, *Erismatura australis*, Gould, which is now in the Collection of the newly formed Launceston Museum. This is the first time the bird has been recorded from Tasmania, its range being previously limited to New South Wales, Victoria, South and West Australia, over which it is rather sparingly dispersed.

Through the liberality of the same gentleman, the Trustees of the Australian Museum have just received the skin of a male New Zealand Shoveller, *Spatula variegata*, Gould, that was obtained amongst others of the same species by Mr. Thomas Carr, on the 20th of June, 1892, at One Tree Point, on the river Tamar near Launceston; numerous individuals of which were seen in the neighbourhood during the past winter. This species may be distinguished from the *Spatula rhynchotis* of Australia and Tasmania, to which it is closely allied, by being less robust and slightly smaller in its admeasurements; the feathers of the lower portion of the neck and mantle are white instead of fulvous brown, the short scapulars also have a larger amount of white on them, and the elongated scapulars are plume-like and more conspicuously marked with a broader lanceolate satiny-white stripe. The single male bird received from Mr. Walter Mantell in 1856 upon which Gould founded the species is evidently an exceptional one, if his figure of it in the "Supplement to the Birds of Australia," pl. lxxx. be correct; it shows a far larger amount of white upon the lower portion of the neck, mantle, scapulars, and breast than specimens since obtained in New Zealand or the one at present under consideration; the latter being similar in size and slightly brighter in colour to a mounted specimen in the Museum, obtained from the North Island of New Zealand, and approaching nearer to the figure given by Sir Walter Lawry Buller in his Birds of New Zealand, 2nd edition, Vol. ii. pl. xliii. p. 269, which he stated has been taken from a "fine male ... in the best condition of plumage." With the specimen sent from Tasmania, a box containing a number of small fresh-water shells was forwarded, marked "taken from the gullet of *Spatula variegata*," and which I have handed to my colleague Mr. John Brazier for examination, who has determined them to belong to the following species:—*Tatea rufilabris*, A. Adam, found in Tasmania, South Australia, Victoria, New South Wales, and Queensland; *Bithynella simsoniana*, Brazier, and *Assiminea bicincta*, Petterd, both peculiar to Tasmania.

Dr. P. Herbert Metcalfe, the Resident Medical Officer at Norfolk Island has also forwarded to me for identification, the skins of three birds which he obtained on that island during April and May of this year, one a fully adult specimen of the White Heron *Herodis egretta*, Gmelin (*H. syrmatophorus*, Gould), which has an extensive geographical distribution, having been recorded over the greater portion of the Old World, the Malay Archipelago, New Guinea, Australia, Tasmania and New Zealand; the little Black Cormorant *Graculus sulcirostris*, Brandt, inhabiting the Australian and Austro-Malayan Region, and the White-headed Stilt, *Himantopus leucocephalus*, Gould, occurring likewise in Australia, the Austro-Malayan Region, and New Zealand; the latter is not in fully adult plumage, and shows an admixture of smoky black feathers intermingled with the white on the crown of the head and occiput, a not uncommon variety in this species in its first season's plumage, a similar one having been obtained last year on behalf of the Trustees of the Australian Museum by Mr. T. R. Icely, the Visiting Magistrate at Lord Howe Island; also a specimen of the Black-billed Spoonbill, *Platalea melanorhyncha*, Reichenbach, found also in Northern, North-eastern, and North-western Australia, both of which have not previously been recorded from that island. In the early part of this month another specimen of *Himantopus leucocephalus* was presented to the Trustees by the Rev. Joseph Annand, M.A., of Tangoa, Santo in the New Hebrides, with a label attached—"Obtained at Tangoa, Santo, May 4th, 1892, not common here," showing that this interesting nomad has during a very short period been found in three hitherto unrecorded and widely separated localities.

On FURTHER TRACES of *MEIOLANIA* in N. S. WALES.

By R. Etheridge, Junr., Palæontologist.

In 1889 I described* the first, and so far the only remains of this remarkable genus discovered in N. S. Wales, from the Canadian Lead, Gulgong. The fossils consisted of a small horn-core, greater part of a caudal vertebra, and two annular segments of the tail-sheath. Irrespective of the interest attached to the extended geographical distribution, lies the fact of the much more important geological range, perhaps even indicating a distinct species of the animal.

Evidence is now to hand, in the form of two horn-cores, of the existence of *Meiolania* in the superficial deposits near Coolah. The specimens form part of a small collection, consisting of bones of *Diprotodon, Phascolonus, Procoptodon,* &c., lately presented by Mr. J. McMaster, of Coolah. The conical processes almost rival in size those of the original *Meiolania Owenii*, Smith-Woodw. Mr. McMaster states that the fossils were found in the new channel of the Oaky Creek, branch of the main Weetalabah Creek, and in another branch known as Binnia Creek. The Weetalabah flows into the Castlereagh River, in the Bligh District, County Napier, about twenty-two miles north-west of Coolah.

The conical processes, in their present state of preservation, when placed on their broad bases, are more or less oblique—one more so than the other—thick bosses, graduating to moderately sharp apices, with an indefinitely quadrate rather than a strictly trihedral section. The peripheral or basal outline is imperfect.

In the smaller of the two horn cores, or conical processes, the longest basal diameter, *i.e.*, in the direction of the obliquity, is four inches ; the greatest transverse breadth at right angles to the former is three inches ; the height, taken vertically from the base to the apex, is fully three inches ; whilst the length of the longest, or anterio-apical ridge (for it seems that in the tail-sheath of *Meiolania Owenii*, figured by Owen,† the longest ridge of the conical processes is always anterior), is three and a half inches.

---

* Records Geol. Survey N.S. Wales, 1889, I., pt. 3, p. 149.

† Phil. Trans., clxxii., t. 65.

Assuming this to be correct, one of the faces of the trihedral process, the dorsal, is flattened, or in the slightest degree convex ; the under, or ventro-lateral, being faintly concave, and the posterior flattened and to some extent truncate. The apex is sharp, acuter than any of the processes figured by Sir R. Owen,[*] but less generally cornute than the supra-temporal cores *b* of the head.[†]

The second specimen only differs materially from the first in the antero-apical line losing much of its ridge-like character, and becoming obtusely rounded. Owing to the more extensive preservation of this part of the process, and the disintegration of the posterior lower portion, this horn-core presents the appearance of a greater obliquity than the other. The length of the antero-apical obtuse ridges is four inches ; the antero-posterior diameter is four and a half inches ; the transverse diameter three inches ; and the height two and three-quarter inches. The lateral and posterior faces are flattened. The surface of both cores is pitted and veined by neuro-vascular markings.

If, in the first place, it be admitted that these are osseous cores for the support of dermal appendages, their interpretation does not seem surrounded with much difficulty. We are not acquainted with any Australian extinct animal, other than *Meiolania*, possessing such exoskeletal outgrowths; and as we know only the skull, part of the tail-sheath, and a few individual bones of this genus, it is but logical to compare these bony processes with those of either one or other of the former.

The horn-cores of the skull in *Meiolania* are either depressed mammillary (the supra-parietal and other smaller pairs), or acutely conical and cornute (the supra-temporal pair). Those of the tail-sheath, on the other hand, arranged in four parallel rows, two dorsal and two lateral, are "massive conical processes, like the horn-cores of the skull, but of larger size, being broader and thicker in proportion to their length, and rather more robust at the apex;"[‡] the upper or dorsal pair being the largest and longest. The appearance of our fossils would indicate that they are from the rings of a tail-sheath, although on comparison with a good plaster reproduction of *M. Owenii*, they are seen to be more strictly trihedral, and their apices more regularly conical and sharper than in the former. The difference in shape may perhaps be more apparent than real, and arise in a great measure from their detached condition and imperfect peripheries ; although at present their bases are wider in proportion to the height than in

* Phil. Trans., clxxi., t. 37 ; *Ibid*, clxxii, t. 65.
† Phil. Trans., clxxi., t. 37, f. 1, *b*
‡ Phil. Trans., clxxii., p. 547.

M. Owenii, and the angle of inclination they would probably form, with the median line of the tail, is different. So far the conviction of the Writer is that they are horn-cores of a *Meiolania*, probably detached from a tail-sheath and possibly from a species differing from those described.

The late Sir R. Owen united in his description of the tail-sheath of *Meiolania Owenii*, the two rings and cap* with a detached ring.† He remarked‡ "The anterior ring . . . . may have come from a more advanced part of the tail, but the peripheral border of the hinder aperture . . . . fits that of the front aperture of the foremost of the coalesced group." Before me are excellent plaster reproductions of these fossils, and with the highest possible respect for the weighty opinion of the late celebrated Author, it appears to me that this opinion has been too hastily formed. Judging from the casts in question, made I believe, at the Natural History Museum, London, portions between the two parts must be missing, for the union is anything but a happy one. The conical processes on the detached ring are much smaller than the anterior pair on the coalesced portion of the tail-sheath, the curvature of the processes is unlike, and to some extent the angle they form with the median line of the tail is different. Now the assumption naturally would be that the more anterior in position, the larger the processes; and for the reasons cited I am of opinion that the two portions appertain to separate individuals. One other point may be mentioned in support of this. In the tail-sheath of coalesced processes the lateral pair almost pass insensibly below into the ventral surface, but in the detached ring there is a considerable interval of almost vertical walls between the preserved lateral process and the ventral surface.

We look forward to the day when, between the various National Collections, it will be possible to put together a tolerably perfect skeleton of this curious animal.

---

* Phil. Trans., clxxii., t. 65, f. 1–3 *(pars.)*
† Phil. Trans., clxxii., t. 65, f. 1.
‡ Phil. Trans., clxxii., p. 547.

NOTES ON AUSTRALIAN AQUATIC HEMIPTERA.

(No. 1.)

By Frederick A. A. Skuse, F.I.S., Entomologist.

(Plate XI.)

The following are descriptions of two species of fresh-water Hemiptera, found commonly in the vicinity of Sydney, and which appear to be novelties. As opportunity occurs, the author hopes to supplement them with diagnoses of further species inhabiting the fresh-water creeks and ponds of New South Wales, and, if possible, of those of the neighbouring colonies :—

Family HYDROMETRIDÆ.

Genus Hydrometra, *Fab.*

HYDROMETRA AUSTRALIS, *sp. nov.*

(Plate xi. fig. 3.)

Above black or olive-black, shining ; beneath yellowish-grey with a silvery bloom. Head with two longitudinal orange-yellow lines connected on the hind margin, and an orange spot or short line before the eyes. Antennæ black ; first joint about one-third the length of the whole taken together. Pronotum parallel, coniform posteriorly, bordered with an orange-yellow line, and with a longitudinal line traversing about one-sixth of its length, and two very short (sometimes indistinct) longitudinal lines anteriorly ; obtusely tuberculated anteriorly. Pleuræ and coxæ striped or spotted with orange-yellow. Elytra wanting. Abdominal segments with a more or less distinct interrupted median orange-yellow line.

Length.—8 mm.

Hab.—Sydney, N.S.W.

Family LIMNOBATIDÆ.

Genus Limnobates, *Burm.*

LIMNOBATES STRIGOSA, *sp. nov.*

(Plate xi. figs. 1, 2.)

Long narrow, brown or yellowish-brown ; head about the length of the thorax, subcylindrical, widened in front; eyes hemispherical, set in the sides of the head considerably behind the middle. First joint of the antennæ half the length and twice the thickness of the second. Abdomen at its widest part scarcely wider than the thorax. Tarsi black.

Length.—11 mm.

Hab.—Sydney, and Botany Swamps, N.S.W.

— — —

Appended are brief notes of species known to occur in this country :—

Family NOTONECTIDÆ.

Genus Corixa, *Geoff.*

Three species of *Corixa* common in the ponds about Sydney.

Genus Sigara, *Fabr.*

Two species, rather abundant.

Genus Anisops, *Spin.*

Anisops australis, Stal. Ofr. K. V. Ak. Forh. xii. 190 ; Stal. Eug. Resa, 267.

Several other species abundant.

Family NEPIDÆ.

Genus Nepa, *Linn.*

Nepa tristis, Stal. Ofr. K. V. Ak. Forh. xi. 241 ; Eug. Resa. 266.

Hab.—Waterloo Swamps, N.S.W.

Genus Ranatra, *Fabr.*

Ranatra filiformis, Fabr. Skrivt. Nat. Selskal. i. 228 ; Ent. Syst. iv. 64 ; Syst. Rhyn. 108 ; Schneid. Neu. Mag. i. 31 ; H. Sch. Wanz. Ins. ix. 31, pl. 290, fig. II ; Stal. Hem. Fabr. 2, 135.

Generally distributed.

Genus Belostoma, *Latr.*

Belostoma indica, Stoll. Pun. 34, pl. 7, fig. 4 ; St. Farq. et Serv.
Enc. x. 272 ; Serv. Hist. Hem. 429 ; Mayr. Verh. z. b.
G. Wien. xxi. 426.

Generally distributed.

Genus Diplonychus, *DeLap.*

Diplonychus eques, L. - Duf. A. S. E. F. 4me Sér. ii. 394 ; Mayr.
Verh. z. b. G. Wien. xxi. 437.

Hab. Australia.

Diplonychus rusticus, Stoll. Pun. 36, pl. 7, fig. 6 ; Sulz. Alg.
Gesch. Ins. 92, pl. 10, fig. 2 ; Fabr. Syst. Rhyn. 106 ; L.
Duf. A. S. E. F. 399 ; Mayr. Verh. z. b. G. Wien, xxi. 438.

Generally distributed.

Genus Naucoris, *Geoffr.*

Occurs commonly ; several species known, but none described.

Family HYDROMETRIDÆ.

Genus Hydrometra, *Fabr.*

Hydrometra cursitans, Fabr. Syst. Ent. 729 ; Sp. Ins. ii. 377 ;
Mant. Ins. ii. 308 ; Syst. Rhyn. 259 ; Stal. Hem. Fabr. i.
131.

Hab. Australia.

Hydrometra australis, sp. n.

Hab. Sydney, N.S.W.

Two or three undescribed species are known.

Genus Halobates, *Esch.*

Halobates wüllerstorffii, Frauenf. Vchr. z. b. G. Wien, xvii. 458,
pl. 12, figs. 1, 2, 6, 8, 10 ; Chal. Rep.

Hab. Coast of Australia ; Port Jackson ; Western Australia.

Halobates whiteleggei, Sk. Records Aust. Museum, Vol. i. No. 8,
p. 175, pl. xxvii.

Hab. Port Jackson.

Obs.—George H. Carpenter, Asst. Naturalist to the Science
and Art Museum, Dublin, has recently characterised a species,
H. regalis (Proc. Roy. Soc. Dublin, xv. p. 144, pl. xiii. figs. 1 - 8),
from examples obtained by Prof. A. C. Haddon off the shores of
the island of Mabuiag, Torres Strait, which closely resembles

H. whiteleggei; but having mutually examined specimens of each, we have ascertained that *H. regalis* is constantly much the larger insect in both sexes, and that there exist characters in the front tarsi and male genital organs which prove that Mr. Carpenter's species is sufficiently distinct to deserve a different name.

Family LIMNOBATIDÆ.

Genus Limnobates, *Burm.*

Limnobates strigosa, sp. n.

Apparently of wide range.

REMARKS ON A NEW *CYRIA* FROM NEW SOUTH WALES.

BY FREDERICK A. A. SKUSE, F.L.S., Entomologist.

[Plate XI. figs. 5 - 10.]

COLEOPTERA.

BUPRESTIDÆ.

Cyria, *Solier.*

THE form figured (pl. xi. figs. 5 - 10) represents a new species of *Cyria* originally proposed to have been described in the present paper, but recently named by the Rev. T. Blackburn (Trans. Roy. Soc. S. Aust. xv. i. p. 41, 1892) as *C. tridens,* from a specimen received from this Museum. The series of about a dozen examples was originally obtained by the author from Mr. W. Smart, of Manly, who procured them from an amateur collector on the Richmond River, N.S.W. By some mistake Mr. Blackburn also fails to mention the locality or source from which he received the specimen from which his description was derived. Fig. 4 represents *C. imperialis,* Don., in contrast with the present insect.

GEOLOGICAL AND ETHNOLOGICAL OBSERVATIONS
MADE IN THE VALLEY OF THE WOLLONDILLY RIVER,
AT ITS JUNCTION WITH THE NATTAI RIVER,
COUNTIES CAMDEN AND WESTMORELAND.

By R. ETHERIDGE, JUNR., Palæontologist.

[Plates XII., XIII.]

THE following observations were made during a short visit, in
company with Mr. W. A. Cuneo, Station-master at Thirlmere, to
the junction of the Wollondilly and Nattai Rivers, to further
examine some interesting phenomena noticed during a previous
visit by the latter gentleman. The localities in question form a
portion of the district of Burragorang, "a local name for that
part of the Wollondilly valley which occurs between the junction
of the Nattai and the Cox with the former river."[*]

The Wollondilly Gorge is about twenty miles from Thirlmere,
and the descent into the valley commences at the highest point
of the route, known as "The Mountain," or in the Aboriginal
language as Queahgong. This point is 1,900 feet above sea-level
(approximately)[†] and the descent, by a magnificently engineered
although most costly zig-zag road, is very rapid and steep; and
the river being itself only about one hundred and fifty feet above
the sea, this allows of a fall on the road of at least 1,700 feet.
Queahgong, as the crow flies, is only one and a quarter miles
from the Nattai junction.

Both the Wollondilly and the Nattai have cut deep gorges
through the Hawkesbury Sandstone, into the Coal-measures and
Upper Marine beds of the Premo-Carboniferous beneath it. The
Hawkesbury Sandstone forms a perpendicular face of rock, a
sharp escarpment in fact, whilst the united Coal-measures and
Upper Marine present a fine slope down to the alluvial flats,
in places bordering the river. By the combination of these

---

[*] W. B. Clarke, Quart. Journ. Geol. Soc., 1866, xxii., p. 443.

[†] The late Rev. W. B. Clarke gave the height of the highest point in
his section of Burragorang as 1,996 feet, but I do not think it was taken
exactly at this spot. (See Sed. Form. N. S. Wales, 4th edit., 1878, 2nd
section).

geological formations, and the effects of the elements upon them, some of the boldest and most picturesque scenery in New South Wales is produced, rivalling even that of the Blue Mountains. At this point the gorge from escarpment to escarpment is not more than two miles wide, if it amounts to that. Particularly grand is the view, when the visitor, standing on any of the upper sharp turns of the road, looks up the valleys of the Wollondilly and Nattai above the junction; and probably one of the grandest outlines of the whole is that of the huge hill,* which frowns over the point of union of the two rivers.

During the descent of the Queahgong road, and during the ascent a few days later, I endeavoured to trace a junction line between the Hawkesbury Sandstone and Coal-measures, in connection with the unconformity believed to exist between the two, but the base of the scarp is so piled with huge blocks, and covered with *débris*, and dense vegetation, that no clear section can be seen. The same difficulty seems to have impeded the Rev. W. B. Clarke, years ago, when he explored this valley, for he remarks : "At the base of the Hawkesbury rocks, blocks fallen and accumulated so as to hide the junction. Dense vines, fig-trees, ferns and jungle, with pools of water." About nine hundred to 1,000 feet down, or from seven to eight hundred feet above the river, shales make their appearance, interbedded with quartz conglomerates of the Hawkesbury Sandstone. Shales continue until about 1,300 or 1,400 feet have been reached on the descent, and it is somewhere between the two points indicated that the actual junction takes place.

The Hawkesbury Sandstone consists of a coarse sandstone, yellow, red, or of purplish tints in colour, becoming very pebbly and conglomeritic towards the base. The bedding is practically horizontal, and the joints are numerous, causing displacements in large masses of rock.

The first coal seam is met with at from 1,300 to 1,400 feet below the summit, or about three to four hundred feet above the river, at no great distance from the junction of the two series of rocks. In Clarke's section the uppermost coal seam is given as at about nine hundred and fifty feet above sea level, or seven hundred and fifty feet above the Wollondilly. Mr. Cunco has obtained *Glossopteris* in these measures.

The only published information with which I am acquainted relating to this particular portion of Burragorang, besides Clarke's "Section" already referred to, is a paper by the same Author

---

* I may here remark on the paucity of names attached to such grand physical features in many districts, particularly the present one, and how conducive to exact physical and geographical description some well-devised scheme of nomenclature would be.

"On the Occurrence and Geological Position of Oil-bearing Deposits in New South Wales."[*] In this essay Clarke correctly indicated the position of the Upper Marine beds at the bottom of the section, and remarked on their resemblance to the Muree Series of the Hunter River Coal-field, and on their supporting "a series of coal-measures, which are capped by Hawkesbury rocks, all resting apparently in a nearly horizontal position on each other."[†] This horizontality is very remarkable, and a most noticeable feature, and renders it still more difficult to determine the supposed unconformability, although its position may possibly be marked by the occurrence of springs. At the same time Clarke mentions that at the immediate junction of the Nattai and Wollondilly, the lowest beds (Upper Marine) are seen dipping slightly to the west. The highest elevation attained by the Upper Marine beds is five hundred feet he says, opposite the mouth of the Nattai; and this is above sea-level, not above the level of the river bed. On the Mount Queahgong section these beds seem to attain a rather higher level, in fact on the eastern side of the gorge the strata all appear to occupy a somewhat higher position.

Spirifers and *Stenopora*, according to Clarke, occur in the Marine beds, but I was not able to visit the fossiliferous spots through want of time. At Singleton, however, on the Hunter River, *Stenopora* occurs in rounded bomb-like calcareous nodules. Now, in the Upper Marine beds, behind Queahgong House (Mr. Maurice Hayes'), on the western bank of the Wollondilly, heavy nodules of a calcareous sandstone occur, resembling cannon-balls, having nuclei of calcareous matter, but not *Stenopora*, or other fossils, so far as I saw; otherwise the resemblance to the Singleton nodules is very strong. Lines of pebbles are also seen in these beds, and at times solitary pebbles occur in the ball-like segregations, although not necessarily central.

No intrusions of igneous matter, as described by Clarke higher up the Nattai Valley, and by the late Mr. C. S. Wilkinson near Mittagong,[‡] in a similar series of rocks, were observed.

Kerosene Shale has been found at several places in the valley in the Upper Coal-measures, but has not been worked successfully so far.

The Rev. W. B. Clarke, speaking generally of this magnificent valley, says "Nothing can so clearly mark the origin of the deep ravines by continuous washings and erosions (probably after some dynamical action had fissured the country), as the fallen blocks of the plateau, and the pebbles which cover the face of the country

---

[*] Quart. Journ. Geol. Soc., 1866, xxii., pp. 439-448.
[†] Ibid, p. 443.
[‡] Ann. Report Dept. Mines N.S. Wales for 1881 [1882], p. 141.

in the line of drainage."* May it not be possible that the starting point of the Burragorang Valley was some great earth-movement, possibly connected with the great faultings which "probably took place towards the close of the Tertiary epoch,"† one of which, known as the Lapstone Hill fault, assisted in the formation of the abrupt eastern margin of the Blue Mountains?

With regard to more recent deposits, many of the gullies running up through the Upper Marine beds, and the Coal-measures, exhibit small waterfalls, around which are deposited considerable masses of calcareous tufa.

————

The Aborigines of the Wollondilly and Nattai Valleys, must, from local accounts, have existed in considerable numbers, and are now only represented by interments, carved trees, wizards' hands, and charcoal drawings in rock shelters along the precipitous escarpments.

The first objects investigated under this head were the "Hands-on-the-Rock," which had been reported by Mr. Cuneo. The "rock" consists of a huge mass of Hawkesbury Sandstone (Plate XII) about seventeen feet in breadth and length, hollowed out on the side overlooking the river to the extent of six feet. It is perched on the side of a gentle rise from the Wollondilly, having rolled from the higher ground above, and alongside the track from the Nattai Junction to Cox's River, in the immediate south-west corner of the Parish Werriberri. The cavernous front of the rock is fifteen feet broad, and twelve feet high. On the back wall are depicted a number of red hands, both right and left. The principal ones, arranged roughly in a sigmoidal curve, are reproduced in Plate XII, with the extended fingers invariably pointing upwards. The other hands are irregularly scattered to the right and below those just referred to, and altogether there may be as many as seventeen. Under the principal hands are four white curved bands, resembling boomerangs or ribs, the whole of the hands being relieved, as is usually the case with these representations, by white splash-work. The hand-marks in this shelter differ, however, from any I have seen before by an unquestionably previous preparation of the rock surface for their reception by incising the surface to the shape of each hand, thus leaving a slightly raised margin around each. I have recently given† an epitome of our knowledge of these hand imprints, their method of preparation, and supposed significance sufficiently full to render any further reference unnecessary at

————

* Quart. Journ. Geol. Soc., 1866, xxii., p. 445.
† C. S. Wilkinson, Notes on the Geol. N.S. Wales, 2nd Edit., 1887, p. 70.
‡ Records Geol. Survey N.S. Wales, 1892, iii., Pt. i., p. 34.

present.   The colour red, amongst black races, was the symbol of
evil.*

Mr. Maurice Hayes, of Queahgong, informed me that he has
known the rock for the past fifty years, and that the imprints
have not altered in the least.   He found it difficult to obtain
reliable information from the Aborigines regarding them ; they
expressed ignorance, but ultimately gave him to understand that
the "hands were the imprints of those of their Deity, when on
earth."

The large alluvial flats in this neighbourhood, along the Wollondilly, were, I was informed, great gathering grounds for the
various tribes from many miles round, even those of Goulburn
and Shoalhaven participating.

On a spur overlooking one of these green expanses, known as
Gorman's Flat, immediately at the junction of the Wollondilly and
Nattai Rivers, in Portion B. 171/587, Parish of Wingecarrabee,
County Westmoreland, we investigated an interment, thirty years
old, indicated by a single carved tree, but the device has, I regret
to say, been wantonly destroyed.   This grave is known to be
that of "Jimmy Aremoy," or "Blackman's Billy," of the local
tribe, and called in the Aboriginal dialect *Ah-re-moy*, and was
covered by a small mound at the foot of a small tree, forty-seven
feet north of the carved tree, and had been surrounded by a
sapling fence.   After removing† the mound and superincumbent
soil, we found the grave had been filled with boulders and large
pieces of rock, to the depth of four feet six, whilst under this was
a layer of split timber and bark.   On removing this, we found
the skeleton well wrapt in what had once been an old coat, a
blanket, and an opossum rug.   The skeleton was doubled up in
the usual manner, the arms drawn up to the breast, and the legs
against the abdomen, placed on the right side, and facing the
south-east.   On endeavouring to remove the remains, the whole
collapsed, and it was found possible to secure only the skull and
limb bones.   The whole of the bones were blackened and much
decayed, from the presence of a good deal of soakage water.   Mr.
Maurice Hayes told me that the local Aborigines generally buried
in a sitting posture, the corpse being in a small drive from the
bottom of the grave proper—the Theddora Tribe, at Omeo, buried
in a similar manner; and with a stake driven through the
skull from above; but in this case the deceased had certainly

* Fraser, Journ. R. Soc. N.S. Wales for 1882 [1883], xvi., p. 213.

† The grave was opened with the permission and assistance of Mr.
Maurice Gorman, the owner of the ground.

‡ Howitt, Journ. Anthrop. Inst. Gt. Brit. and Ireland, 1884, xiii.,
p. 190.

been laid in the prone positon. Not the least interesting fact was the variety of articles placed with the deceased, according to aboriginal custom. Loose in the superincumbent earth we found an ingenious conversion of a piece of forked iron into a probable spear-head, a pointed stick, and some loose pieces of timber. Underneath the skeleton in various positions there occurred an old comb in two pieces, a thimble, a large iron spoon, the blade of another spoon, a small bullet mould, handle and portion of the tin plate-work of an old "quart-pot" or "billy-can," fragment of a clay tobacco pipe-stem, top of an old metal powder or shot-case, containing shot and a few shirt buttons, and last, but by no means the least curious, a castor oil bottle, still containing what seems to be a portion of the oil, —this was placed directly under the head.

Mr. Maurice Gorman subsequently conducted us across the Wollondilly to a slight rise above "Larry Gorman's Fat," Parish of Nattai, on the Nattai side of the Wollondilly, County of Camden, and a little below the junction of the rivers. Here we viewed the burial place of a "Chief" of the late local tribe, the interment having taken place about fifteen years ago. It lies contiguous to one of three marked trees placed in a triangle, the longest side or base of the latter being half a chain in length, and bearing north-west and south-east. The trees are still erect, although the carvings are more or less obliterated by bush fires, but they seem to have been chiefly in zig-zag lines, and of course cut with an iron tomahawk. The heavy rain prevailing at the time deterred us from investigating this burial. It is situated on either Portions C. 98/70 or C. 98/105, Parish of Nattai.

This concluded our investigations in Burragorang proper, but on returning to Thirlmere, we diverted our course near Vanderville, across the Werriberri Creek to "The Hermitage," the estate of Mr. W. G. Hayes, Parish of Burragorang, County of Camden. Through the kindness of Mr. Hayes we were allowed to examine a much more extensive burial-ground than either of the preceding. Here, on a small plateau above and to the east of the Waterfall Creek, a branch of the Werriberri, and behind, or to the south of the homestead, are four graves of various sizes distinguished by four carved trees, more or less in a state of dilapidation. There does not appear to have been any geometrical form of arrangement assumed in the placing of these graves, unless it be a roughly rhomboidal one. We expected, from current report, to find five graves here, but four only rewarded our efforts. Three of the graves and three carved trees are more or less in a north-west and south-east line. Starting at the north-west corner, the figures on a She-oak (*Casuarina*) have been partially obliterated, ten feet from this is the first grave, and fourteen feet from the latter is another carved She-oak (Plate

XIII., Fig. 1), now lying on the ground and much decayed. Fifty-one feet still further on occurs the largest grave, and at another fifty-one feet the third ornamented tree, a dead gum still standing but much burnt by bush fires, and bearing an extraordinary figure (Plate XIII., Fig. 2). Between the last grave and this tree, and deviating somewhat from the straight line in the third interment, at right angles to the original starting point ; and fifty-four feet from it, at right angles, is the fourth carved tree, also a dead gum, bearing the figures shown in Plate XIII., Fig. 3. At right angles to this again, and distant sixty-four feet, is the fourth grave, apparently without any indicating tree near it. We did not investigate the contents of these graves owing to want of time.

The carving on the first tree (Plate III., Fig. 1) is four feet four inches long, and one foot seven inches wide ; that on the second tree (Plate XIII., Fig. 2) is five feet six inches long, and one foot ten inches wide; and that on the third (Plate XIII., Fig. 3) is the smallest, three feet three inches long by nine inches wide, as now preserved.

In the Waterfall Creek previously referred to, are numerous grooved surfaces on the rock-bed and sides, caused by the process of tomahawk grinding.

I am not acquainted with any systematic account of Australian carved trees; in fact little seems to have been collectively written about them, and very few representations figured. Probably some of the earliest illustrations are those by Oxley, Sturt, and " W.R.G.," presumed to be from the context of his writings, Mr. Surveyor W. R. Govett, of Govett's Leap fame. Oxley discovered a grave on the Lachlan, consisting of a semi-circular mound, with two trees overlooking it, barked and carved in a simple manner.[*] These carvings consisted of herring-bone on the one tree, and well marked curved although simple lines on the other. The explorer Sturt noticed an oblong grave beyond Taylor's Rivulet, Macquarie River, around which the trees were "fancifully carved on the inner side," one with a figure of a heart.[†] The anonymous author (W.R.G.) describes an occurrence of this kind at Mount Wayo, County Argyle, in the following words, " The trees all round the tomb were marked in various peculiar ways, some with zig-zags and stripes, and pieces of bark otherwise cut."[‡] A Mr. Macdonald states that the Aborigines of the Page and Isis, tributaries of the Hunter River, carve serpentine lines on two trees to the north-west of each grave.[§]

---

[*] Journ. Two Expeds. Interior N.S. Wales, 1820, p. 130, plate.

[†] Two Expeds. Interior S. Austr., 1834, I., p. 14.

[‡] Saturday Mag., 1836, IX., No. 279, p. 184.

[§] Journ. Anthrop. Inst. Gt. Brit. and Ireland, 1878, VII., p. 256.

The figures are either composed of right lines or curves, more commonly the former, but a few instances have been recorded of natural objects, such as the outline of an Emu's foot, seen by Leichhardt on a gum tree in the Gulf Country.* One thing is self-evident, such carvings possessed a dual if not a triple significance. We have already seen the employment of them to indicate an interment, presumably acting the part of a tomb-stone, for it is believed by some that the figures on a tree in each case correspond to those on the inner side of deceased's 'possum rug, the *mombarai*, or "drawing," which Fraser thinks was distinctive in each family, or a peculiar modification of the tribal *mombarai*.† So far as I can gather, such devices invariably indicated the last resting-place of a male. Mr. E. M. Curr states‡ that the Breeaba Tribe, at the head-waters of the Burdekin River, North Queensland, employed marked trees to commemorate a battle. He figures a tree from the banks of the Diamantina, barked and marked by a series of close, irregularly super-imposed notches, like those made by a Black when climbing a tree. These, however, can hardly be compared to carvings.

According to Mr. J. Henderson, Dr. John Fraser, Mr. A. W. Howitt, and Mr. Macdonald previously mentioned, Bora Grounds are also embellished with carved trees. The first-named describes§ the approach to one of these initiation places at Wellington as through "a long, straight, avenue of trees, extending for about a mile, and these were carved on each side with various devices. . . At the lower extremity of this, a narrow pathway turned off towards the left, and soon terminated in a circle." Mr. Henderson further remarks that the fact of the use of this place for Bora purposes was communicated to him by the then head-man of the tribe. Dr. Fraser says‖ that the Gringai Tribe, one of the northern N.S. Welsh tribes, clear two circular enclosures, one within the other, for their Bora, and that the trees growing around the smaller circle are carved "with curious emblematical devices and figures"; whilst Mr. Macdonald informs us that on the Bora ground of the Page and Isis River Natives, as many as a hundred and twenty marked trees occur round about.¶ Confirmation is further afforded by Mr. W. O. Hodgkinson, who saw a Bora ground on the Macleay River with "trees minutely tatooed, and carved to such a considerable altitude that he

* Journ. Overland Expol. Moreton Bay to Port Essington, 1847, p. 356.
† Journ. R. Soc. N.S. Wales for 1892 [1893], xvi., p. 201.
‡ The Australian Race, 1886, ii., p. 433.
§ Obs. Colonies of N.S. Wales and V.D. Land, 1832, p. 145, pl. 3.
‖ Journ. R. Soc. N.S. Wales for 1882 [1883] xvi., p. 205.
¶ Journ. Anthrop. Inst. Gt. Brit. Ireland, 1878, vii., p. 256.

could not help feeling astonished at the labour bestowed on the work."[*]

If, as previously stated, according to current report, the designs on the trees be the same as those on the 'possum rugs, the transfer of them to the trees surrounding a grave must have had some important and lasting meaning to the survivors. The figures on the rug may have indicated some degree of ownership, a crest, coat of arms, or monogram, as it were, and in such a case the reproduction on the trees surrounding a grave may be looked upon as an identification of the deceased. Henderson speaks of the tree carvings as symbols. "A symbol is afterwards carved upon the nearest tree, which seems to indicate the particular tribe to which the individual may have belonged."[†] Or had they a deeper esoteric meaning, one only known to the learned men of the tribe? Smyth states[‡] that the figures on the inner sides of the 'possum rugs "were the same as those on their weapons, namely, the herring-bone, chevron, and saltier." How easily these same devices can be traced, in a general way, both on the carved trees and some of the wooden weapons, is amply shown by many of the excellent figures given in Smyth's work. This painstaking Author, in briefly dealing, too briefly in fact, with this interesting subject, says,[§] "The natives of the Murray and the Darling, and those in other parts adjacent, carved on the trees near the tombs of deceased warriors *strange figures having meanings no doubt intelligible to all the tribes* in the vast area watered by these rivers." By the Kamilaroi[‖] they were regarded as "memorials" of the dead.

It is much to be regretted that before the last remnant of this fast disappearing race has passed away, a translation, or at any rate an explanation of these matters, cannot be obtained.

* Smyth, Aborigines of Victoria, 1878, I., p. 292.
† Obs. Colonies of N.S. Wales and V.D. Land, 1832, p. 149.
‡ Aborigines of Victoria, 1878, I., p. 288.
§ Ibid, p. 286. The italics are mine.
‖ T. Honery, Journ. Anthrop. Inst. Gt. Brit. and Ireland, 1878, vii., p. 254.

PHOLAS OBTURAMENTUM; AN UNDESCRIBED BIVALVE FROM SYDNEY HARBOUR.

BY C. HEDLEY, F.L.S.

[Plate XIV.]

IN the course of a critical examination of various Mollusca from Port Jackson, specimens of the only *Pholas* reported thence passed under review. This species has hitherto been accepted as *P. similis* by all writers and collectors who have occupied themselves with the marine mollusca of our coast. This identification appears to have originated with G. F. Angas, who in his "List of additional Species of Marine Mollusca to be included in the Fauna of Port Jackson and the adjacent Coasts of New South Wales,"* enumerates as species 93 :—

"BARNEA SIMILIS. *Pholas similis*, Gray, MS. Brit. Mus.; Thesaurus Conch, pl. ciii., f. 12 – 14 ; 'Bottle and Glass' rocks, in sandstone (Brazier)."

This entry is repeated verbatim by Mr. T. Whitelegge in the "List of the Marine and Freshwater Invertebrate Fauna of Port Jackson and the Neighbourhood."† Mr. Brazier informs me that this determination was also supported by the late G. B. Sowerby.

Prof. Tate records *Barnea similis*, Gray,‡ as "burrowing in clay at low tide mark, Port Lincoln, St. Vincent Gulf, and south-east coast [of South Australia]; also in Tasmania."

On examining the statement of Angas closely, our faith in his accuracy is weakened by observing that Gray's name was not, as he states, a manuscript one. It was first published with a description in 1835 in the Appendix to Yates' New Zealand, p. 309, and it again appeared, with further information, eight years later, in Vol. ii. of Dieffenbach's New Zealand, p. 254 where the author remarks that it is "very like *Pholas parvus*, but larger, broader, and more acute in front."

Between the New Zealand and the Australian species a discrepancy at once appears on comparing examples of the Port

---

* Proc. Zool. Soc., 1871, p. 99.

† Journ and Proc. Roy. Soc. N.S.W., xxiii. (1889), p. 234.

‡ Trans. Roy. Soc. S. Australia, ix., p. 80.

Sept. 1893]

Jackson *Pholas* with the figures illustrating the former (Thesaurus Conchyliorum, Vol. ii., pl. ciii., ff. 12, 13, 14).* Having no examples of the New Zealand species at my disposal, I am constrained to base my remarks on these engravings, which, from their finish, should be faithful representations. Sowerby's mistake in supposing the species to be an undescribed one, implies that he had Gray's types before him; while both Philippi's diagnosis of *P. antipodum*† and Gray's description answer well to these drawings and also leave no room for doubt that the specimens were actually obtained in New Zealand.

Viewed from the ventral side the difference is most apparent, the gape extending a third further along the ventral margin, and being much wider anteriorly in Sowerby's figure than in the local species; *P. similis* may be likened to a cylinder cut obliquely at an angle of 30° and *P. obturamentum* to one cut at an angle of 45°. Dorsally the profile of the New Zealand form appears to be more swollen and to taper more sharply at the anterior extremity than does the Australian. The spinose ridges would seem to be more feebly developed, and the size to be smaller in the local species; but, without more material for comparison, the writer would not attach specific importance to such characters. The Sydney shells, having been procured from sandstone rock, may reasonably be supposed to be smaller and smoother than if their burrows had been drilled in softer substances.

The next ally of our species seems to be *P. manilensis*, Philippi,‡ next to that the British *P. parvus*, Pennant, and least of the three the New Zealand *P. similis*. The unfigured Papuan *P. beccarii*, Tap. Can.§, probably is akin.

These five appear to represent a small and natural group, among which the Australian species is clearly distinguishable by the more anterior position of the beaks and by the less posterior extension of the gape.

This species may be characterised as follows:—

PHOLAS OBTURAMENTUM, *sp. nov.*

Shell somewhat tongue-shaped, evenly tapering from the beaks to the posterior extremity, rounded posteriorly, dorsal and ventral margins straight, gibbous ventro-anteriorly, the closed valves including a heart-shaped space rather longer than wide; valves in

---

* Except Philippi's Abbild. Beschr. Conch., Vol. iii., *Pholas*, pl. i., f. 3., the other published figures, viz., Conch. Icon., Vol. xviii., *Pholas*, pl. iii., f. 10, and Conch. Cab. (2) Vol. xi., pt. xx., pl. vi., f. 3, are mere copies, the latter a bad one, of Sowerby's f. 12.

† Zeits. Mal. iv., 1847, p. 71, &c.

‡ Thes. Conch. pl. ciii., ff. 17, 18.

§ Ann. Mus. Civ. Genova, vii., p. 1032.

contact along the ventral margin for half the length of the shell, the left valve slightly overlapping the right. Colour a uniform dull white. Epidermis pale straw colour, largely abraded, thin and very wrinkled. Sculpture about thirty concentric growth laminæ in the interstices of which are two or three raised hair lines; anteriorly these laminæ are puckered up into lines of square-headed thorns by transverse waves radiating from the beaks. Opposite the beaks the thorny ridges diminish for a few series and cease, posteriorly they are represented by faint wrinkles on the growth laminæ. Beaks situated at a quarter of the length of the shell from the anterior extremity. Hinge margin narrow, sharply recurved, not appressed to the valve and destitute of such denticles as possessed by *P. dactylus*. Dorsal plate lanceolate, single, entire, striated by divaricating growth lines, with a shallow median furrow. Subumbonal process long, flat and curved. Length 40, height 20, breadth 16 mm.

Attached to some specimens are pale brown, tough, coriaceous siphon sheaths.

Type.—In the Australian Museum, Sydney.

The specimens on which my description is based were collected by Mr. Brazier in a small outcrop of shale at Vaucluse Bay. That gentleman informs me that he also encountered the species at "The Nobbys," near Newcastle, and at the mouth of the Bellinger River, some examples attaining twice the dimensions of those now recorded.

NOTES on AUSTRALIAN *TYPHLOPIDÆ*.

By Edgar R. Waite, F.L.S.

1. Typhlops curtus, *Ogilby*.

It is worthy of remark that no one in Australia has hitherto investigated the *Typhlopidæ* of the continent: the reason probably lies in the fact that only a very small portion of this immense area can be said to be at all adequately known, and scientific workers have ample material of more attractive and better differentiated forms than characterise the *Typhlopidæ*. Although of all snakes this group is admitted to be the most difficult of determination, some fifteen Australian species are known; all these have, however, been described in Europe: by Gray and

Boulenger in London, Peters in Berlin, Schmidt in Hamburg, Schlegel in Leyden, and Jan in Milan : consequently all the type specimens are in Europe, and without direct reference to these the task of determination is no light one; it is, however, a pity that such valuable material as the large collection of local *Typhlopidæ* contained in the Australian Museum should remain year after year uninvestigated, and in taking up the examination of these specimens I therefore propose to publish any points of interest with which I may meet, in the hope that it may be a step in the direction of placing our knowledge of the Australian *Typhlopidæ* more on a level with better worked families.

The Collection in the Museum, although large, is, as might naturally be expected, somewhat local, being composed mainly of individuals collected in New South Wales, more particularly in the neighbourhood of Sydney. As only a few of the species described have been obtained from this Colony, any specimens from other parts of Australia with which we might be favored would be especially valuable.

In this connection I may mention that the Trustees of the Macleay Museum, Sydney, have very kindly granted me permission to examine the extensive collection of *Typhlopidæ* formed by the late Hon. Sir William Macleay ; and Mr. C. W. de Vis has generously offered to place in my hands, for investigation, the examples contained in the Queensland Museum of which he is the Curator.

Only one species has, I believe, been described in Australia, and it is therefore disappointing to have to point out its identity with a species previously described.

In all the *Typhlopidæ*, so far as I am aware, the body scales are arranged in an *even* transverse series. In the "Records of the Australian Museum," Vol. ii., p. 23, Mr. J. Douglas Ogilby describes a species under the name of *Typhlops curtus*, and remarks that it has twenty-*three* series of scales round the middle of the body. This apparent departure from the usual conditions led me to re-examine the type specimen, when I found the number to be twenty-*four*. The species must therefore be referred to *Typhlops ligatus*, Peters,* with which it agrees in every particular. Peters obtained his specimen from Port Mackay. Ogilby's type is from Walsh River, Gulf of Carpentaria, and I have found in the Museum Collection other examples from Coomooboolaroo, Dawson River. Therefore, so far as is known, this species is confined to Queensland.

[I have submitted the foregoing note to Mr. Ogilby, who entirely agrees with my remarks, and was not aware of Peters' paper when he wrote his description.]

---

* Monatsb. d. K. Akad. d. W. Berlin, 1879, p. 775, fig. 3.

2. TYPHLOPS RÜPPELLI, *Jan.*

[Plate XV., Figs. 5 and 6.]

It may occasion some little surprise that I seek to raise to specific rank a species which is generally considered as identical with *T. nigrescens*, Gray. This species is common in New South Wales, and has a more or less conspicuous dark patch on each side of the body near the anus.

In commencing an examination of the large collection of Australian *Typhlopidæ* in the Museum, I made a careful study of *T. nigrescens*, and came to the conclusion that Peters was correct in regarding it and *T. rüppelli* as one and the same species.* During further investigation, however, I have discovered examples which are so entirely distinct that I have no longer any doubt as to the specific position of *T. rüppelli*.

When describing this species, Jan remarks† that it is especially characterised by a round black spot on each side of the anus. In no example of *T. nigrescens* which I have examined is the spot darker than the body scales, and only in extreme cases does the color at all approach it. Moreover the coloration is confined to three scales at most, and on account of the shortness of the tail appears very close to the extremity of the body. (Plate xv., fig. 5). In *T. rüppelli* the spot is extremely conspicuous, is absolutely jet black and infinitely darker than any of the body scales. It is of large size, occupying several scales, and owing to the greater relative length of tail is at some distance from the extremity of the body. (Plate xv., fig. 6).

The relative length of the tail is one of the most striking points of difference. In *T. nigrescens* it has about twelve scales and is broader than long (Jan says a quarter longer than broad), while in *T. rüppelli* there are about twenty-five scales, and the length is fully twice the breadth. The former species is of more robust form, has the posterior part of the body much thickened and attains larger dimensions, reaching 570 millim.; while the latter is of more even diameter and smaller, none of our specimens exceeding 340 millim.

The scales on the head do not differ very materially: in *T. rüppelli* the internasals approach more nearly together, and the portion of the rostral between them is rather more acute than in *T. nigrescens*. This is indicated in Jan's figures,‡ but as pointed

* Monatsb. d. K. Akad. d. W. Berlin, 1865, p. 262.
† Icon. Gén. des Ophidiens, p. 14.
‡ *Ibid*, 9 Liv., pl. i., figs. 1 and 2.

out by Peters with regard to *T. preissi* and other species* they are not absolutely reliable.

It appears highly probable that Peters had never seen an example of *T. rüppelli* when he stated its identity with *T. nigrescens*, but like Prof. McCoy† had considered that Jan described the species from an example of *T. nigrescens;* probably one in which the anal spots were well marked.

3. TYPHLOPS PROXIMUS, *sp. nov.*

[Plate XV., Figs. 1 - 4.]

Habit stout, thickened posteriorly. Snout very prominent, with acute margin. Rostral more than half the width of the head, extending almost to the level of the eyes, narrowed in front and below ; the portion visible from beneath longer than wide ; nasal incompletely divided, the fissure extending from the first labial to the upper surface of the snout ; nostrils inferior, close to the margin of the snout ; preocular narrower than the ocular ; nasal the widest. Eye very distinct, situated in the angle between the preocular and supraocular. Internasal, supraoculars and parietals enlarged. Four upper labials. Diameter of the middle of the body thirty-five times in the total length. Tail, not longer than broad, terminating in a short stout spine. Twenty scales round the body.

Colors.—Variable in spirits, generally brownish-olive to greyish-brown above, each scale margined with yellow, lower surfaces yellow ; sometimes a more or less distinct small brown patch on each side of the anus.

Dimensions.

Total length	...	... 405·0	millim.
Length of head	...	... 8·5	,,
Width of head	...	... 8·5	,,
Width of body	...	... 11·5	,,
Length of tail	...	... 8·0	,,
Width of tail	...	... 11·0	,,

Habitat.—New South Wales and Victoria. Several specimens.

Type.—In the Australian Museum, Sydney. Reg. No. 6411.

There should be no difficulty in distinguishing *T. proximus* from the other Australian species ; the character of the nasal fissure being in contact with the first labial and produced on to the upper surface of the snout is common only to three other species,

---

* Archiv. für. Naturg. 1862, p. 35 (not 1861, Zool. Record, i.)

† Prod. Zool. Victoria, ii., p. 9.

namely, *T. nigrescens*, Gray, *T. reginæ*, Boulenger,—each of which has twenty-two transverse scales and a rounded snout—and *T. ligatus*, Peters, readily recognisable by the narrow rostral and the twenty-four rows of scales. In *T. proximus*, as already mentioned, the snout is decidedly acute, and the scales are arranged in twenty series. In Plate xv., figs. 3 and 4 are drawn from the type specimen, and figs. 1 and 2 from an average example of *T. nigrescens* introduced for the purposes of comparison ; in the latter, four body scales are in contact with each parietal, while in *T. proximus* there are only three, owing to the smaller number in the transverse series. The figures being drawn to the same scale (four times natural size) it will be seen that the head of this species is relatively larger than that of *T. nigrescens*, for the specimens are of practically equal length, being 405 millim. and 395 millim. respectively.

It will be noticed that Jan's figures* are fairly accurate, and McCoy, although describing *T. nigrescens*, has figured† at any rate the head of the species I here determine.

Since the foregoing was in type, I have written to Professor Sir Frederick McCoy, and mentioned how closely his figure resembles *T. proximus ;* and although in the text he states that the body scales are in twenty-two rows, I ventured to ask him to re-count the rows in the specimen figured, and I quote the following from his reply :—" First I must thank you for drawing my attention to a misprint,—in my description of *Typhlops nigrescens* in my Prodromus of the Zoology of Victoria, Dec. xi.,—of twenty-two scales instead of twenty, which I find in my MSS. and in all the specimens..." He further mentions that in his figures (Plate 103, figs. 1a. and 1c.) the rostral is not drawn quite sufficiently prominent; this would increase the similarity between his figures and mine, and as he assures me that all the figures on the Plate were drawn from the same specimen (although, owing to the apparent discrepancy in the number of body scales, I had suggested to him that they were not), it appears evident that Plate 103 illustrates *T. proximus* and not *T. nigrescens*. The anal spot is, however, more conspicuous than in any of my specimens, but is subject to much variation, being absent in some examples.

As Prof. McCoy mentions that all his specimens possess the character of having only twenty rows of scales on the body, it would appear that there are no examples of *T. nigrescens* in the National Museum, Melbourne, and we may therefore provisionally infer that this species does not occur in Victoria, and while it is very

---

* Icon. Gén. des Ophidiens, 9 Liv., pl. i., fig. 1a., *et seq.*
† Prod. Zool. Victoria, ii., pl. 103.

common in New South Wales, *T. proximus* is, on the other hand, comparatively rare. Owing, however, to the very limited number of observations made upon the Australian *Typhlopidæ*, it would at present be extremely unwise to hazard many remarks upon their distribution.

DESCRIPTION OF A NEW SHARK FROM THE TASMANIAN COAST.

By J. Douglas Ogilby.

CENTRINA BRUNIENSIS, *sp. nov.*

Centrina bruniensis, Morton (*in lit.*)

Body oblong, with the back and sides rounded, and the belly flattened. Head small and strongly depressed, its breadth equal to the distance between the tip of the snout and the spiracle : snout short and obtuse, the distance between its tip and the nearest point of the mouth less than that between the same and the anterior margin of the eye. Nostrils equidistant from the eye and the extremity of the snout. Eye large, with a strong bony supraorbital ridge, situated midway between the tip of the snout and the anterior gill-opening. Spiracles large, opening behind the upper half of the eye, with a moderate intervening space. Mouth small and transverse, with the lateral groove very broad and deep. Upper jaw with a patch of small, conical, curved teeth anteriorly, consisting of about four irregular rows ; a single series of much larger, erect, compressed, minutely serrated, scalpriform teeth in the lower jaw. Gill-openings small, the posterior one pierced immediately in front of the base of the pectoral fin. The first dorsal commences above the middle gill-opening, and rises by a continuous and equal gradation to the spine, its outer margin being straight ; behind the spine the rise is much more abrupt, and the contour is slightly convex with the tip rounded ; the posterior margin is deeply concave ; the height of the fin beneath its extremity is equal to the distance between the anterior gill-opening and the tip of the snout, that of the spine equal to the head in front of the spiracle ; the spine is situated in the anterior portion of the last fourth of the base of the fin, is perfectly

straight, with a slight inclination forwards, and protrudes a short
distance beyond the membrane; its base is exactly midway
between the tip of the snout and the origin of the caudal,
while the distance between the bases of the two dorsal spines is
but little more than the length of the base of the first dorsal in
front of its spine, and five-sevenths of the length of the fish in
front of it; the intradorsal ridge is very strongly developed; the
second dorsal has a general resemblance in shape to the first, but
is not so large; the upper margin is more regularly even, and the
extremity, which is much more pointed, hangs vertically above
the base of the caudal, instead of falling within the vertical from
its own base, as with the anterior fin; the length of its base is
equal to that of the intradorsal space, and to the height of the
fin beneath its tip, and is four-sevenths of the outer margin; the
spine is situated in the latter portion of the anterior half of the
fin, and is gently curved backwards throughout its entire length;
in height it is but little less than that of the first dorsal; the
pectoral fin is well developed and pointed, its length equal to the
space which divides its anterior basal margin from the nostril;
the distance between its base and that of the ventral is two-fifths
longer than that between the dorsal spines, and is traversed by a
strongly developed lateral ridge; the ventral fin commences beneath
the spine of the second dorsal, and the distance between its termination and the origin of the lower caudal lobe is equal to
that between the second dorsal and the caudal fin; the caudal
lobes are well developed; the outer margin of the upper lobe is
straight, the angle and the posterior margin rounded; the lower
lobe is triangular, with the anterior margin slightly concave, and
equal in length to the posterior margin, which is sinuous, with the
angle rounded. The skin is covered with small rough scales, each
of which bears a well developed spinate projection, which consists
of a central spine from which radiate four compressed wings, each
one terminating at its outer angle in a somewhat shorter spine
than the central one.

Color.— Uniform sandy brown.

The Shark described above was sent to the Australian Museum,
by the authorities of the Tasmanian Museum, Hobart, for identification and preservation, and was placed in my hands for description
previous to being returned. The specimen was picked up on the
shore of Bruny Island, Tasmania, in a dried state, but on being
relaxed was found to be in a fair state of preservation. The
enormous height of the dorsal fins, and their contiguity, the one
to the other, separates this species at a glance from *C. salviani;*
the scales also differ considerably.

Type.—In the Tasmanian Museum.

The specific name has been given to it at the request of Mr.
Alex. Morton, Curator of the Tasmanian Museum.

DESCRIPTION OF A NEW PELAGIC FISH FROM NEW ZEALAND.

By J. DOUGLAS OGILBY.

Some months ago the Australian Museum received, through the kindness of the Fresh Food and Ice Company, Sydney, a fine specimen of an unknown pelagic fish from New Zealand, being one of a consignment forwarded to the Company for sale in Sydney, the bulk of which consisted of Trout, Rock Cod (*Percis colias*), and Flounders (*Rhombosolea monopus*). This example, having been imported for edible purposes, had of course been thoroughly cleaned before being placed in the ice chamber, and I am therefore, unable to give the number of pyloric appendages.

The occurrence of this genus in Australasian waters, is quite as interesting as the discovery of *Tetragonurus*[*] some years ago at Lord Howe Island, and bears a close analogy to it, both genera being more or less distinctly Mediterranean types.

CENTROLOPHUS MAORICUS, *sp. nov.*

B. vii. D. 38. A. 25. V. 1/5. P. 21. C. 19.

The length of the head is equal to that of the caudal fin, and five and a half in the total length; the greatest height of the body is beneath the longest dorsal rays, and is contained five times in the same. The eye is large, and is surrounded by a prominent naked lid; it is situated near the upper profile of the head, and its diameter is four and one-tenth in the length of the head, and one and one-seventh in that of the snout, which is obtuse and abruptly truncated, and projects slightly beyond the lower jaw; the interorbital space is convex and its width is equal to the length of the snout. The nostrils are situated far forward, immediately behind the angle of the snout; the anterior is oval and vertical, the posterior much larger and subarcuate. The upper profile of the head is slightly concave. The jaws are equal, and the cleft of the mouth is of moderate width, the maxilla reaching to beneath the anterior fourth of the orbit. The vertical limb of the preopercle is straight and slightly inclined forward, its angle and lower limb finely denticulated; the margins of the sub- and inter-opercles rather more strongly so. A single series of cardiform teeth in the jaws, so irregularly placed as to form in many cases an apparently double series. The dorsal fin

---

[*] Macleay, Proc. Linn. Soc. N. S. Wales, x. p. 718, and op. cit. (2) i. p. 511; Ramsay & Ogilby, op. cit. (2) iii. p. 9.

commences a little behind the posterior half of the pectoral, and the length of its base is two and one-fifth in the total length; the anterior rays are short and gradually increase in length to the twelfth which, with the thirteenth and fourteenth, is the longest in the fin, and about one-seventh longer than the snout; behind these the rays become abruptly shorter, so that the outer margin of the fin is concave behind them, and the posterior two or three rays appear to be distinctly elongated, the last being about equal to the eighteenth: the anal commences beneath the middle dorsal ray, and its shape is similar to that of the dorsal, the base of which is exactly twice the length of its base; the fifth ray is the longest, and is but a fraction shorter than the longest dorsal ray, while the distance between the base of the first ray and the origin of the caudal is contained one and one-fourth times in that between the same point and the extremity of the snout: the pectoral is small and rather pointed, the fourth to seventh rays the longest, two and one-seventh in the length of the head: ventrals small, equal in length to the snout: caudal deeply emarginate. Scales very small, each one pierced by a small, central, circular pore; opercle, sub- and inter-opercle scaly, the scales being of equal size to those on the body; rest of the head naked, covered with a thick and densely porous skin; vertical fins scaly over about two-thirds of their height. Lateral line forming a long curve to beneath the longest dorsal rays.

Colors.—Uniform brown, darkest above; the sides of the head washed with dull blue; the fins and opercles with gold.

Type.—In the Australian Museum.

The Australian Museum also possesses a specimen of *Pteraclis velifer*, a species previously unrecorded from New Zealand.

REVIEW OF THE GENUS *SCHEDOPHILUS*, COCCO, AND ITS ALLIES.

By J. Douglas Ogilby.

The present paper was suggested by the occurrence on the coast of New South Wales of a specimen of *Schedophilus maculatus*, this being the first record for the genus from Australian waters, and the time has been deemed opportune to review the history, such as it is, of the various species, the more especially that these pelagic forms are liable to occur at any time upon any part of the

Australian coast, and, where so little is known of them, it is advisable that no opportunity should be lost of recording any fresh facts in connection with their distribution and mode of life.

The genus *Schedophilus* was originally placed by Günther among the *Coryphænina*, at that time considered to be a Group of the *Scombridæ*, but subsequently accorded family rank. The discovery, however, off the Pacific coast of North America of two closely allied forms, induced Professors Jordan and Gilbert to remove these fishes, respectively known as *Icosteus enigmaticus* and *Icichthys lockingtoni* to a separate family, for which they proposed the name *Icosteidæ*, and in which was included the *Bathymaster* of Cope, a genus which differs in a much greater degree from the typical *Icosteus* than does *Icosteus* from a typical *Schedophilus*, which latter genus is apparently omitted entirely from the family; the words of those authors, after diagnosing the *Icosteidæ*, being: "This group, as at present constituted, is composed of three very diverse genera, each of a single species, inhabiting the deeper waters of the North Pacific. It is probably most nearly related to the *Malacanthidæ*, from which it is distinguished by the presence of pyloric cœca, and by the non-labrid dentition."[*]

The formation of a new family for these fishes, and the consequent disruption of his *Coryphænidæ*, does not meet with Dr. Günther's approval, and he further holds that the splitting up of Cocco's genus is distinctly untenable; he remarks: "I fail to find in the description (of *S. lockingtoni*) characters which would warrant a generic separation from *Schedophilus*, or the creation of a distinct family *Icosteidæ*."[†] With the latter part of this opinion we are entirely in accord, for we cannot consider that such characters as the dentition and the absence of pseudobranchiæ, however useful in separating genera, can with propriety be applied to the differentiation of families.

With reference to the generic distinctions pointed out by Lockington, Jordan, and Gilbert, we cannot, however, so readily give in our adherence to Dr. Günther's views; such characters as the presence or absence of scales, of groups of epidermal spines, and of an airbladder[‡] being of sufficient importance to make us hesitate before declining to accept the genera *Icosteus* and *Icichthys* proposed by the American ichthyologists. In this communication we shall, however, include all the known species under the common term *Schedophilus*, using the other names as signifying

---

[*] Synopsis, p. 619.

[†] Voy. Challenger, xxii. p. 46.

[‡] This is apparently of less importance, and is of course well known in the true Mackerels.

natural subdivisions of the genus, which, when our knowledge of these pelagic forms is more thorough, may or may not be raised to full generic rank.

SCHEDOPHILUS.[*]

Schedophilus, Cocco, Giorn. Innom. Mess. Ann. iii. 1829.

Crius, sp. Valenc. in Webb & Berthel. Iles Canar. Poiss. p. 45, 1836.

Icosteus, Lockington, Proc. US. Nat. Mus. ii. p. 63, 1880.

Icichthys, Jordan & Gilbert, Proc. US. Nat. Mus. ii. p. 305, 1880.

Schedophilopsis, Steindachner, SB. Ak. Wien, lxxxvi. p. 82, 1882.

Branchiostegals six or seven : pseudobranchiæ present. Body oblong-ovate or ovate, strongly compressed. Cleft of mouth moderate. Preopercle spiniferous. A single series of small teeth in the jaws : vomer, palatines, and tongue edentulous. One dorsal fin, extending nearly along the whole back, formed by flexible rays, the anterior of which are more or less simple : anal similarly formed : ventrals thoracic, with one spine and four or five rays. Scales small and cyclid, or absent ; vertical fins with a basal scaly sheath. Airbladder present or absent.

Geographical Distribution.—Mediterranean ; tropical and subtropical parts of the Atlantic and Pacific Oceans ; not as yet recorded from the Indian Ocean, nor from the East Coast of America.

Synopsis of the species.

A. Scales small ; branchiostegals seven ; ventral fins with five
   soft rays .... (ICICHTHYS)

   a. Scales striated ; dorsal commencing above the margin of
   the opercle ....*I. maculatus.*

  aa. Scales smooth.

   b. Dorsal commencing behind the head.........*I. lockingtoni.*

    Dorsal commencing above the vertical margin of the
   preopercle ....*I. bertheloti.*

---

[*] Agassiz gives, as the derivation of Cocco's generic name, σχέδη *scheda,* and φίλος, *amicus.* The former of these words means a leaf or tablet, and has therefore no significance in connection with the fish ; if, however, the name be derived from σχεδία, the meaning of which is a raft or float, a recognised habit of the young *Schedophili* would be felicitously expressed.

B. Scales minute; branchiostegals six or seven. (SCHEDOPHILUS)

    a. Lateral line smooth; ventral fins with five soft rays, inserted
        in front of the base of the pectorals.......*S. medusophagus.*

C. Scales absent; branchiostegals six......................(ICOSTEUS).

    a. Lateral line armed with groups of small spines; ventral
        fins with four soft rays, inserted behind the base of the
        pectorals..*I. enigmaticus.*

In the above synopsis I have been obliged to place *S. bertheloti*
along with *S. lockingtoni* and *S. maculatus,* because of the comparatively large size of the scales—as shown in Dr. Steindachner's
figure—in comparison with those of *S. medusophagus,* as pourtrayed
in Dr. Günther's figure, and as were present, if my memory serve
me, in my Irish example of that species.

SCHEDOPHILUS MACULATUS.

Schedophilus maculatus, Gnth. Catal. Fish. ii. p. 412, 1860, *and*
    Journ. Mus. Godeffr. Fisch. p. 148, 1876.

Schedophilus marmoratus, Kner, SB. Ak. Wien, liv. p. 366,
    1866.

B. vii. D. 9/27. A. 3/23. V. 1/5. P. 19. C. 17. L. lat. 105.
    L. tr. 22/47.

Length of head equal to its height at the hinder margin of the
orbit, and 3·33 in the total length (without caudal); height of body
2·20 in the same. Eye large, with the supraorbital ridge well developed and overhanging, its diameter 3·10 in the length of the
head, and equal to the interorbital space, which is almost flat; snout
very short and obtuse, its length 1·50 in the diameter of the eye.
Jaws equal: cleft of mouth moderate and oblique, the maxilla
reaching to the vertical from the middle of the eye. Upper
profile of the head rising almost vertically from the premaxillaries,
thence sloping to the occiput, which, with the nape, is strongly
convex, and compressed into a moderately sharp ridge. Both
limbs of the preopercle armed with strong spines, those at the
angle being the longest, and having their extreme tips curved
upwards; those on the vertical limb straight, but directed
dorsally: sub and interopercles spiniferous, the spines of the
latter more strongly developed. Body oblong-ovate, and strongly
compressed. A single series of small, rather distant, hooked
teeth in the jaws. The dorsal fin commences above the margin
of the bony opercle; its nine anterior rays are distinctly spinous;
the last the highest, a little higher than the diameter of the eye;
beyond the spinous portion the rays increase gradually in height
to the middle of the fin, from whence they descend as gradually
to the last, which is five sixths of the ninth spine, the outer

margin of the fin forming a gentle curve: the anal commences beneath the sixteenth dorsal ray, its origin being a little nearer to the tip of the snout than to the middle of the base of the caudal, and ends a trifle further back than the dorsal; its spines are stronger than those of that fin, the third the highest, two thirds of the dorsal spine: ventral well developed, inserted beneath the base of the pectoral, the second ray the longest, five sevenths of the distance between its origin and the vent, and five ninths of the length of the head; the spine is strong, equal in length to the third anal spine: pectoral rounded posteriorly, two thirds of the length of the head: the least height of the caudal peduncle is three fourths of its length.   Scales small, cyclid, concentrically striated: cheeks, opercles, and occiput scaly; rest of head covered with a thick skin; a series of small pores surrounding the eye: bases of all the fins deeply scaly.   Lateral line gently curved to beneath the posterior fourth of the dorsal fin, thence straight.

Colors.—Ground color pale yellowish brown, so densely covered with deep reddish brown blotches and bands, as to appear only as short, oblique or longitudinal stripes; dorsal fin with seven, anal with four blackish basal spots, which in the former are continued on to the rays above the basal sheath; in the latter are connected by a narrow band running along the outer margin of the sheath; caudal yellowish, with two large basal and three larger median dark brown spots.

Habitat.—Chinese Seas; South Seas; Coast of New South Wales.

The specimen from which the above description was taken, was obtained some years ago on Manly Beach by Mr. Henry Prince, and was, with his usual generosity, presented by him to the Australian Museum.   Though washed ashore, it was in good condition, the only injury being a slight one to the tips of the caudal rays.

The length to the broken rays is three inches and a half.

SCHEDOPHILUS LOCKINGTONI.

Icichthys lockingtoni, Jordan & Gilbert, Synops. Fish. N. Am. p. 621, 1882.

Schedophilus lockingtoni, Gnth. Voy. Challenger, xxii. p. 46, 1887.

B. vii.   D. 40.   A. 28.   V. 1/5.   L. lat. 120.   Cœc. pyl. 6.

Length of head 5·00, height of body 4·00 in the total length. Eye moderate, longer than the snout, its diameter 4·00 in the length of the head.   Lower jaw prominent: cleft of mouth

---

* Derived from εἴκω to yield, and ἰχθύς a fish, in allusion to the flexible skeleton.

moderate, slightly oblique, the maxilla, which is slender and scarcely widened at the tip, concealed beneath the preorbital, and extending to beyond the vertical from the front margin of the pupil. Upper profile of head slightly convex, the snout abruptly descending. Preopercle with radiating striæ, each of which terminates in a flexible point: opercle and subopercle crossed by similar striæ. Body oblong and somewhat compressed. Teeth in the jaws minute, sharp, closely and evenly set. The dorsal fin commences nearly midway between the vent and the origin of the ventrals; all the rays are soft and, with the exception of the first, branched; the anterior rays very low, the fin gradually rising posteriorly, the highest rays 3·00 in the length of the head: the anal fin commences slightly in front of the middle of the body, and ends just in front of the last dorsal ray : ventral short and small, inserted a little behind the pectorals, with one of the rays slightly filamentous, its length 3·00 in that of the head : pectorals rounded, small, not so long as the head : caudal broad and fan-shaped, the peduncle slender. Scales small, soft, and smooth, in one or two series on the preorbital.* None of the fin rays armed with spinules. Lateral line nearly straight, smooth. Airbladder wanting.

Colors.—Brown, paler below, somewhat punctulated.

Habitat.—Deep water off the coast of California.

Length seven inches and a half.

SCHEDOPHILUS BERTHELOTI.

Crius† berthelotii, Valenc. in Webb & Berthel. Iles Canar. Poiss. p. 45, pl. ix. f. 1, 1836.

Schedophilus berthelotii, Gnth. Catal. Fish. ii. p. 412, 1860.

Schedophilus botteri (Heck.) Steindachn. SB. Ak. Wien, 1868, lvii. p. 379, pl. ii. f. 2.

D. 36-38. A. 23-25. V. 1/5. P. 21. Cœc. pyl. 6.

Length of head‡ 3·75, height of body 3·00 in the total length. Eye large, its diameter 2·60 in the length of the head: snout short, but little more than half the diameter of the eye: interorbital space flat, 1·33 in the same. The maxilla extends to beneath the middle of the orbit. Snout very strongly convex; occiput convex; a shallow concave interspace. Preopercular teeth numerous, rather short,

---

* Other scales on the head, if any, lost on the typical example.

† From κριός, a ram.

‡ Calculated from Dr. Steindachner's description of a young example. I have not been able to consult Messrs. Webb & Berthelot's work, while Dr. Günther's notice, owing probably to the only specimen available to him being a half-grown skin, is valueless for comparison.

those on the vertical limb not *(according to Steindachner's figure)* directed upwards; the denticles of the interopercle moderately strong. Body oblong-ovate, compressed. Teeth in a single series, longer, less numerous, and blunter than in *S. medusophagus*, but similarly curved. The dorsal fin commences above the vertical margin of the preopercle: ventral well developed, inserted almost entirely in front of the base of the pectoral, and reaching as far as the first anal ray; its length 1·25 in that of the head. Scales small, cyclid.

Colors.—Body reddish violet, the head brownish; entire body sprinkled with numerous dark violet dots, the trunk having in addition ill defined blackish cross-bands, or band-like transverse spots, which extend on to the basal portion of the dorsal and anal fins; caudal with cross-bands posteriorly.

Habitat.—Canaries; coasts of Spain and Dalmatia.

SCHEDOPHILUS MEDUSOPHAGUS.

Schedophilus medusophagus, Cocco, Giorn. Innom. Mess. Ann. iii. No. 7, p. 57, 1829; Bonap. Faun. Ital. Pesc. c. fig.; Gnth. Catal. Fish. ii. p. 412, 1860, *and* Journ. Mus. Godeffr. Fisch. p. 149, 1876, *and* Trans. Zool. Soc. xi. p. 221, pl. xlvii. 1881; Steindachn. SB. Ak. Wien, 1868, lvii. p. 377; Lutken, Spol. Atlant. pp. 525, 602, pl. ii. fig. 9 *(juv.)* 1880; Gill, Science, i. p. 117, 1883; Day, Brit. Fish. ii. 1884, Add. p. 367 outline figure i. p. 120; Ogilby, Proc. Roy. Dub. Soc. p. 515, 1885.

B. vi.-vii.   D. 45-50.   A. 27-29.   V. 1/5.   P. 18.   C. 21.

Length of head equal to its height, and rather less than 4·00 in the total length (without caudal); height of body, 2·66 in the same. Eye situated immediately below the upper profile of the head, its diameter nearly as long as the snout, which is obtuse, and 4·00 in the length of the head: interorbital space convex, 1·25 in the diameter of the eye. Lower jaw projecting: cleft of mouth of moderate width and oblique, extending to the vertical from the front margin of the eye; the maxilla rather narrow, widening towards its extremity, reaching to beneath the middle of the orbit. Both limbs of the preopercle armed with short spines, the upper ones on the vertical limb being a little the longer and directed obliquely upwards: interopercle spiniferous, the sub-opercle less so: opercle membranous; its upper portion with radiating osseous striae, which project beyond the margin. Body elongate-ovoid, and strongly compressed. Teeth minute, implanted in a single series on the sharp edge of the jaws. The dorsal fin commences above the root of the pectoral, and terminates at a short distance from the caudal; it is rather low, the longest rays,

which are behind the middle of the fin, not erectile into a vertical
position ; the rays are slender and fragile : the anal commences
a little behind* the middle of the length of the fish, and beneath
the twenty third dorsal ray, and ends a little nearer to the base
of the caudal than does the dorsal ; there is no distinct spinuous
portion to either the dorsal or the anal fin : ventral rather small
and close together, inserted in advance of the base of the pectoral,
its length *(in the figure)* two fifths of that of the head ; pectoral
with a broad base, the upper rays longer than the lower, its
length *(in the figure)* two thirds of that of the head : caudal fin
rounded, rather shorter than the head ; the least height of the
caudal peduncle about equal to its length.   Scales minute, cyclid ;
on the head apparently present on the cheeks only.   Lateral line
curved to beneath the anterior third of the dorsal fin, thence
straight.

Colors.—Pale greenish olive marbled with darker, the markings
being in the form of spots on the upper and of irregular longitudinal
bands on the lower half of the body : vertical fins spotted with
blackish.   Irides nearly white ; a ring of small white pores en-
circling the eye.

This species has been obtained in the Mediterranean, the Mid-
Atlantic, the Pacific near Samoa, on the east coast of Spain, and
on the north-east coast of Ireland, the writer having the good
fortune to secure the last-mentioned example immediately after
its capture.

Length to nine inches and a half.

In Dr. Steindachner's description, the dorsal rays are said to
vary between thirty five and forty seven, which, unless the smaller
number should prove to be a printer's error for forty five, is a
most unusual variation in such a species, and, taken in conjunction
with the fact that some examples were found to have six, others
seven, branchiostegal rays, would go far towards suggesting the
possibility that two species have been confounded together under
the name *Schedophilus medusophagus.*

SCHEDOPHILUS ENIGMATICUS.

Icosteus† *ænigmaticus*, Lockingt. Proc. U.S. Nat. Mus. xxii. p.
    63, 1881 ; Jordan & Gilbert, Synops. Fish. N. Am. p. 620,
    1882; Steindachn. SB. Ak. Wien, lxxxvi. p. 82, 1882; Gnth.
    Voy. Challenger, xxii. p. 46, pl. xliv. 1887.

---

* A little before in Günther's figure in the Transactions (*q.v.*)

† Derived from ἴκω, to yield, and ὀστέον, a bone ; alluding to the
soft and flexible nature of the bones.

*Schedophilopsis** spinosus*, Steindachn. *loc. cit.* lxxxiii. p. 396,
1881.

B. vi.   D. 52-55.   A. 37-40.   V. 1/4.   L. lat. 110-120.

Length of head 5·00 (4·25 without caudal), height of body 3·50
in the total length.   Eye small, its diameter 6·00 – 7·00 in the
length of the head, 1·66 – 1·85 in the length of the snout, and
2·20 – 2·50 in the convex interorbital space.   Jaws equal : cleft
of mouth of moderate width, the maxilla reaching to beneath the
middle of the eye : nostrils small, simple, approximate, situated
nearer to the end of the snout than to the orbit.   Preopercle
with several small spinous processes on the margin.   Body elongate-
ovoid, much compressed ; the upper profile rises abruptly from
the interorbital space, and describes a gentle curve to the end of
the dorsal fin.   Teeth in the jaws in a single series, minute, those
in the lower jaw rather the larger.   The dorsal fin commences
opposite to the base of the pectoral, and terminates on the same
plane as the anal ; the anterior rays are short and unbranched ;
the rays gradually increase in height posteriorly, and the longest,
which are close to the end of the fin, reach nearly to the base of
the caudal : the anal commences opposite to the twenty fourth
to twenty seventh dorsal rays, and is similar in shape to the
posterior half of the dorsal fin : ventral small and narrow, inserted a little behind the base of the pectoral, the second ray the
longest, its length three sevenths of the distance between its
origin and the vent, and four elevenths of that of the head :†
pectoral broad, rounded, the middle rays the longest, equal to the
postorbital portion of the head : caudal rounded, the least height
of the peduncle less than its length, and about 5·50 in the height
of the body.   Scales absent.   Lateral line gently curved above
the anterior rays of the anal, thence straight, clothed along its
entire length with groups of minute spines : all the fin rays with
similar spines.

Colors.—Light yellowish brown, pellucid below the dorsal and
above the anal fins : upper half of head and body ornamented
with large blackish spots, irregular in shape, and smallest on the
head and neck ; they form a series along the base of the vertical
fins, which are similarly spotted.

Habitat.—Pacific coast of the United States, in deep water.

Length up to twelve inches.

---

* From *Schedophilus*, and ὄψις, appearance.
† In the Challenger figure.

ON THE OCCURRENCE OF *BEEKITE* IN CONNECTION WITH
"FOSSIL ORGANIC REMAINS," IN N. S. WALES.

BY R. ETHERIDGE, JNR., Palæontologist.

[Plate XVI.]

Among the many mineral substances replacing the original
carbonate of lime composing what are generally known under
the name of "fossils," are iron-pyrites, iron-oxide, sulphur,
malachite, magnesite, talc, and silica of various forms, such
as *Beekite*, chalcedony, and both common and precious opal.
"By far the commonest mode of replacement is that whereby an
originally-calcareous skeleton is replaced by silica. This process
of 'silicification'—of the replacement of *lime* by *silica*—is not
only an extremely common one, but is also a readily intelligible
one; since carbonate of lime is an easily and flint a hardly
soluble substance. It is thus easy to understand that originally
calcareous fossils, such as the shells of Mollusca, or the skeletons
of Corals, should have in many cases suffered this change, long
after their burial in the rock, their carbonate of lime being
dissolved away, particle by particle, and replaced by precipitated
silica, as they were subjected to percolation by heated or alkaline
waters holding silica in solution."[*]

"In a large number of cases of silicification," continues Prof.
Nicholson, "the minute *structure* of the fossil which has been
subjected to this change is found to have been more or less
injuriously affected, and may be altogether destroyed, even
though the *form* of the fossil be perfectly preserved. This is the
rule where the silicification has been secondary and has taken
place at some period long posterior to the original entombment
of the fossil in the enveloping rock; whereas if the original
fossilisation has been effected by infiltration with silica in the first
instance, then the minute structure is usually perfectly preserved.
In secondary silicification, as seen in corals and shells, the
carbonate of lime of the original fossil is gradually more or less
completely replaced by silica, the process beginning on the exterior and gradually extending inwards."[†]

In New South Wales we are at present acquainted with three
methods of replacement of carbonate of lime—by iron-pyrites,

[*] H. A. Nicholson, Man. Pal., 3rd Edit., 1889, I., p. 7.
[†] *Loc. cit.*, p. 7.

common and precious opal, and "orbicular silica" or *Beekite.*
We have in the Collection a valve of a Tertiary Pelecypod from
Port Fairy, in Victoria, completely converted into iron-pyrites ;
the Collection of the Department of Mines possesses some excellent specimens of conversion into the two opals from the
Western Opal-fields ; whilst in the present communication it is
intended to deal with certain corals, showing the entire structure
replaced by orbicular silica, or *Beekite,* a mineral not recorded in
Prof. A. Liversidge's 'Minerals of New South Wales.'[*]

Beekite, strictly speaking, is not a true mineral species, but a
chalcedonic variety of silica, replacing the carbonate of lime of
fossil organic remains by secondary silicification.   Bristow,[†] who
gives the best description, says that in the New Red Conglomerate
of Devonshire (Eng.), it occurs as rounded masses from half to
one inch, but sometimes from three to six inches.   The surface
consists of chalcedony arranged in tubercles from the size of a
pin's head to that of a pea, each of which is surrounded by one
or more rings, producing a more or less rosette-like appearance.
Amongst other localities, Bristow incidentally mentions its occurrence in India, and "in Australia, in Triassic Conglomerates,"
but I am not acquainted with the source of his information as to
the last-named occurrence.

I have met with *Beekite* on a *Strophalosia* from the Permo-
Carboniferous of Bingera, Co. Murchison, in the Department of
Mines Collection, and plentifully on Siluro-Devonian Corals in
the black limestone of Cave Flat, Murrumbidgee.   If my memory
does not deceive me, there are also traces of the mineral on the
chalcedonically replaced Brachiopoda from the Permo-Carboniferous
rocks of Point Puer, Tasmania, in the Natural History Museum,
London.

Prof. A. H. Church,[‡] who has to a certain extent artifically
simulated *Beekite* in the Laboratory, speaks of it as "a curious
silicified substance, at once a mineral and a fossil," presenting
itself under such a variety of aspects as to baffle description, so
far as regards its physical features.   Its chemical composition,
however, is more constant, the original constituents having
become " so modified in constitution as to contain on an average
no less than 92 per cent. of silica," a small but variable quantity
of lime remaining, but more in the form of silicate than carbonate.
Prof. Church's theory, expressed in his own words,[§] is " that
water charged with carbonic acid and silica removed the carbonate

* The Minerals of New South Wales, etc., with map. (8vo. London, 1888).
† Glossary of Mineralogy, 1861, p. 39.
‡ Journ. Chem. Soc., 1861, XV., p. 109.
§ Journ. Chem. Soc., 1863, XVI., p. 31.

of calcium from corals, shells, etc., and deposited silica in its room, a portion of the calcium compound also being rearranged and re-precipitated."

With the view of showing the size obtained by a single rosette, Prof. Church figures three costæ and intermediate furrows of an ordinary-sized *Pecten*, over which it had spread.

The best examples of *Beekite* in our Collection are a very large *Syringopora* from the Siluro-Devonian Limstone of Cave Flat, and a *Heliolites* from the Wellington Caves. In the former case the whole of the corallite walls are converted into a granular chalcedonic quartz arranged more or less in lines, where the surface is not occupied by the *Beekite* rosettes, which are usually contiguous to one another and touching. Each rosette consists of a central nucleus, surrounded by concentric rings, which seem to slightly imbricate at their edges. As a rule there are two or three rings, but any number may occur up to eight. Here and there, two nuclei with their rings are surrounded or enfolded in larger and outer rings, forming, as it were, double rosettes. The rings are not always continuous, but broken up into circlets of granules ; and the more numerous the circles are, the finer and closer together they become. In a few cases the rosettes appear to have been so rapidly developed as to have become more or less confluent, whereby the regularity of form is in a measure lost. The concentric structure extends through the whole thickness of the corallite walls.

In the *Heliolites* two conditions are apparent. In the first, the entire surface of the corallum, including both autopores and siphonopores, is converted into a series of large rosettes, obliterating totally the two orders of polygonal corallites. In the second case the autopores remain as more or less rounded openings, the siphonoporal ("cœnenchymal") surface being occupied by the rosettes, this being a species of *Heliolites* in which the siphonopores are largely developed.

Two well-marked instances of *Beekite* silicification may be cited for comparison. Prof. James Hall has figured[*] a *Fenestella* from the Upper Helderberg Formation of New York State, in which the whole of the polyzoarium, both interstices and dissepiments, is converted in this way. Another case is that of Dr. F. Toula's figure[†] of *Spirifer striato-paradoxus*, Toula, from the Carboniferous Limestone of Spitzbergen, in which the rosettes are in some respects even better marked than in our specimens.

---

[*] Ann. Report State Geologist of New York for 1882 [1883], No. 2, t. xxxv. (28), f. 18.

[†] Sitz. K. K. Akad. Wissensch. (Math. Nat. Cl.), Wien, LXVIII., Abth. 1, t. 1, f. 2a.

DESCRIPTION of a NEW FLEA *(STEPHANOCIRCUS DASYURI)* from NEW SOUTH WALES; with NOTES OF SOME OTHER INSECT PARASITES known in AUSTRALIA.

By FREDERICK A. A. SKUSE, Assistant in Entomology.

[Plate XVII.]

The specimens from which the appended description has been derived were obtained in numbers by my colleague, Mr. Edgar R. Waite, and myself whilst searching for *Ixodes* on the body of the Australian Tiger Cat, *Dasyurus maculatus*, Kerr.

It must not be entertained that the writer is impetuous to describe isolated species, or is an advocate of the only too prevalent practice. The reason for now so doing is certainly in part excusable, owing to the distinctive character of the insect under notice, but it is more especially done with the view of soliciting *authentic* specimens of the cutaneous Insect, Arachnid and Arachnoid parasites infesting our native Vertebrates, the majority of which will doubtless prove to be plagued with their own peculiar forms.

Very few records appear to have been made of the external parasites of Australian animals, and few of these with reference to their respective hosts. With the view of collecting specimens, it might be pointed out to those in the bush districts having the opportunity, that they may be sought with success upon any animal. Even the fleas themselves have other "fleas" to bite them. Mammals, birds, reptiles, amphibians, and fishes, all have parasites infesting their skin—in most cases species peculiar to themselves; in many, several distinct forms, each of which usually occupies some particular portion of the surface of the body. These pests are by no means confined to insect representatives; indeed the majority belong to the Arachnida. Various species of flies deposit their eggs in the skins of both warm- and cold-blooded Vertebrates, some permanently residing under the hair or feathers in their perfect condition, and gorging themselves with the blood of their victims. Many varieties of fleas *(Aphaniptera)* have been recorded, most of which, under ordinary circumstances, are peculiar to some particular beast or bird. Bugs and lice, of which numerous undescribed forms doubtless exist on our native animals, may be readily collected. Of Arachnids, it is scarcely necessary to direct attention to the ticks, a species of which, *Ixodes hydrosauri*, Denny, occurs upon one of our large lizards. There are also many kinds of minute eight-legged mites, which feed upon various animals, living upon or under the skin.   Among these might be mentioned, for example, the well-known, microscopic, itch mites *(Sarcoptidæ)* and the subcutaneous parasites of birds *(Hypoderidæ)*, usually to be found in great numbers, or "nests," especially in the fatty masses under the base of the wings, adhering to the veins and in other portions.   Species of all these forms are represented in this country, but the material at disposal is insufficient to induce the publication of descriptions at present.

Order APHANIPTERA.

Family PULICIDÆ.

STEPHANOCIRCUS, *gen. nov.*

Body elongate, especially in the female, bristly, noticeably stronger at the anal extremity.   Antennæ capitate, four-jointed; the second joint in female with long bristles extending to the tip of the fourth, in male very short; fourth joint lamellar, apparently composed of nine segments.   Head moderately large; *in the female with an exserted, cap-like patella in the front, strongly pectinated round its posterior margin*, the face also strongly pectinated; in the male the posterior margin of the head only pectinated ; *eyes wanting in the female;* trophi less than the length of the head ; mandibles extremely slender, minutely serrated, encased in four-jointed labial palpi, which they somewhat exceed in length ; lingua extremely slender ; maxillæ elongate, triangular, somewhat exceeding the second joint of the labial palpi, with no apparent apical joint ; maxillary palpi four-jointed, the first and fourth of about equal length, the third shorter and the second the longest, acuminate ; joints of the labial palpi progressively diminishing in length and thickness.   Prothorax in female with a strong pectinate fringe. Legs long, spinous ; coxæ of posterior two pairs with a distinct notch posteriorly at the apex ; femora very minutely and sparingly spined ; tarsi five-jointed, the first, second, and fifth joints long, the third shorter, the fourth shortest, half the length of the fifth ; claws microscopically denticulate.

STEPHANOCIRCUS DASYURI, *sp. nov.*

Length of male 1·90 mm. ; of female 2·80 mm.

Castaneous brown, nitidous.   Head of the male convex above, of female flat.   Eyes of male small, black.   Pectinal fringes and setæ black or dark brown.   Thorax long, in the female nearly the length of the body.   Abdomen about twice as long as broad in the male, shorter in the female, darker castaneous brown in the female, bristly.   Legs of a uniform pale castaneous brown.

Habitat.—New South Wales, on *Dasyurus maculatus*, Kerr.

The species for which the above new genus has been proposed was at first considered by me to be attributable to *Ceratopsyllus* of Curtis, but the absence of eyes, remarkable structure of the head, and the elongate thorax in the female, seem to demand its exclusion from known genera.

Not the slightest trace of eyes could be detected in specimens of the female, after repeated examinations under a ½in. objective. Their rightful position is occupied by a bristly hair. In my opinion the female anchors herself by the spiny corona, and is perfectly blind.

APPENDIX.

DIPTERA (Flies).

Family ŒSTRIDÆ (Bot-flies, Breeze-flies).

Larvæ parasitic on various species of mammals, found under the skin, in the frontal sinus, or in the stomach.

Examples :

ŒSTRUS, *Linn.*

Œstrus ovis, Linn., the sheep bot. (Proc. Roy. Soc. Tasm., p. 258, 1884).

GASTROPHILUS, *Brauer.*

Gastrophilus equi, Fabr., the Horse bot.

Universally distributed.

Obs.—Also a species which is said to attack the natives of N. Australia (Trans. Aust. Assoc. Ad. Sc., p. 535, 1890).

Family OSCINIDÆ.

BATRACHOMYIA, Kr.

Larvæ living beneath the skin of frogs.

Examples :

B. *nigritarsis,* Sk., on *Hyla phyllochroa* (Proc. Linn. Soc. N.S.W., Vol. iv., Ser. 2., p. 175, 1889). Illawarra, New South Wales.

B. *quadrilineata,* Sk., on *Pseudophryne bibronii* (*l.c.*, p. 177). Burrawang, New South Wales.

Family HIPPOBOSCIDÆ.

(Forest-flies, Horse-tick, Sheep-tick, and Bird-flies).

Perfect insects, living beneath the hair of mammals or the feathers of birds.

Examples :

HIPPOBOSCA, *Linn.*

H. *australis,* Guér., host unknown (Voy. de la Coq., ii., p. 302, 1830). Port Jackson, New South Wales.

H. *viridipes,* Walk., host unknown (Trans. Ent. Soc., N.S. iv., p. 235, 1857). New South Wales.

ORNITHOMYIA, *Latr.* (Bird-flies).

O. australasiæ, Wied., host unknown (Auss. Zweif. ii., p. 608, 1830).   Australia.

O. batchiana, Rond., host unknown (Ann. Mus. Cir. Gen. xii., p. 158, 1878).   Grafton, New South Wales.

O. nigricornis, Erich., host unknown (Archiv. f. Naturg. viii., p. 274, 1842).   Tasmania.

O. stipituri, Sch., on the Emu wren, *Stipiturus malachurus*, Lath. (Reise " Novara," Zool. ii., p. 374, 1868).   Sydney, New South Wales.

O. tasmaniensis, Macq., host unknown (Dipt. Exot., 4th suppl., p. 309, pl. 28, fig. 15, 1850).   Tasmania.

MELOPHAGUS, *Linn.* (Wingless " Sheep-tick").

M. ovinus, Linn., on sheep (Trans. Aust. Assoc. Ad. Sc., p. 540, 1890).   Universally distributed.

OLFERSIA, *Wied.*

O. macleayi, Leach., host unknown (Eph. Ins., p. 12, 1817).   Australia.

Family NYCTERIBIDÆ (Wingless " Bat-ticks ").

Some species known, but none yet described from Australia.

APHANIPTERA (Fleas).

Family PULICIDÆ.

Perfect insects parasitic upon warm-blooded animals.

Examples:

PULEX, *Linn.*

P. echidnæ, Denny, on Australian Porcupine, *Echidna aculeata*, Shaw (Ann. Mag. Nat. Hist., xii., p. 315, pl. xxxvii., fig. 6, 1843).   Tasmania.

P. irritans, Linn., the human flea.

P. felis, Linn., on the domestic cat.

P. canis, Linn., on the domestic dog.

Obs.—This species swarms innumerably in certain seasons in sandy situations and in houses, often assuming the nature of a plague.

P. gallinæ, Linn., on the domestic fowl.

STEPHANOCIRCUS, *Sk.*

S. dasyuri, Sk., on the Tiger Cat, *Dasyurus maculatus*, Kerr. Probably generally distributed in Australia.

Type.—In Australian Museum.

ECHIDNOPHAGA, *Oll.*

E. ambulans, Oll., on Australian Porcupine, *Echidna aculeata,* Shaw (Proc. Linn. Soc. N.S.W., i., Ser. 2, p. 172, 1886).

Obs.—Remarkable on account of its inability to jump. Perfectly distinct from *P. echidnæ,* Denny, from the same host. New South Wales.

Type.—In Australian Museum.

HEMIPTERA HETEROPTERA (Bugs).

Family ACANTHIDÆ.

Perfect insects parasitic upon warm-blooded animals.

ACANTHIA, *Fab.*

Example :

Acanthia lectularia, Geoffr., the bed-bug (Catl. Hem. Hetr. Brit. Mus., part vii., p. 43, 1873). Universally distributed.

HEMIPTERA ANOPLURA (Lice).

Family PEDICULIDÆ.

Perfect insect parasitic upon the bodies of warm-blooded animals, often confined to particular portions.

Examples :

PHTHIRIUS, *Leach.*

P. inguinalis, Leach, on the human body.

PEDICULUS, *Linn.*

P. capitis, De Geer, on the human head.
P. vestimenti, Nitzsch, on the human body.

PHILOPTERUS, *Nitzsch.*

Parasitic upon birds.

P. (Lipeurus) variabilis, Nitzsch, on the domestic fowl.

P. (Lipeurus) baculus, Nitzsch, on the varieties of pigeons.

TRICHODECTES, *Nitzsch.*

Parasitic upon mammals.

T. latus, Nitzsch, on the domestic dog.

T. subrostratus, Nitzsch, on the domestic cat.

T. scalaris, Nitzsch, on the ox.

T. equi, Nitzsch, on the horse.

T. sphærocephalus, Nitzsch, on the sheep.

The above list is very incomplete, the object in publishing it being to direct the attention of our "bush" observers to the diversity of additional forms which might be expected by research.

Our knowledge of the native Arachnid and Arachnoid parasites is too meagre, as far as the exact determination of species is concerned, to yet attempt even a preliminary list.

On a Specimen of *CREX CREX*, Shot at Randwick, New South Wales.

By Alfred J. North, F.L.S., Assistant in Ornithology.

Recently Mr. H. Newcombe, Deputy Registrar-General of Titles, presented a freshly shot specimen of *Crex crex* to the Trustees of the Australian Museum. The bird was obtained the previous day, June 14th, 1893, by Mr. Walter Higgs, who was shooting in a scrubby portion of the Rifle Range at Randwick, a well known haunt of the *Rallidæ*. It was an adult female, and upon dissection the ovaries were found to be fairly developed. This species ranges throughout Western Asia, Europe, and the United Kingdom, it also occurs in Northern and North-eastern Africa, and the late Mr. Gurney records it as common during the summer months as far South as Natal, a straggler also being recorded by Mr. Ayres from Cape Colony. It occurs in Asia Minor, Arabia, and Turkestan, and it is stated by Mr. Seebohm to be common as far North and East as the Altai Mountains; also Dr. Sharpe recently records it in a collection of birds from Fao in the Persian Gulf, but it is not included either by Hume or Murray in the Indian avifauna. Stragglers are recorded by Professor Baird to the Eastern coast of the United States, and Dresser, in his Birds of Europe, states a specimen was said to have been once obtained near Nelson, in New Zealand, but on what authority I know not. Sir Walter Buller does not include it in his Birds of New Zealand. Previously this species has not been recorded from Australia, and although possessed of great powers of flight, it is hard to imagine that the specimen obtained at Randwick, should it have succeeded in reaching Northern Australia by the way of India, Sumatra, and Java, would still have wandered so much farther out of its normal range by crossing the continent to South-eastern Australia. The occurrence of this bird within a few miles of Sydney, where a number of foreign birds are frequently brought by the different boats of the Continental Shipping Companies, would tend to strengthen the opinion that the specimen is an escaped cage-bird, but unless it has moulted since it obtained its freedom, the perfect condition of plumage it is in points to the contrary.

The specimen has been mounted and placed in the Collection, where it will be available for future reference ; but for want of further proof it is undesirable at present to include it in the Australian avifauna.

DESCRIPTION of a NEW SPECIES of PARRAKEET, of the GENUS *PLATYCERCUS*, from NORTH-WEST AUSTRALIA.

By Alfred J. North, F.L.S., Assistant in Ornithology.

PLATYCERCUS OCCIDENTALIS, *sp. n.*

Adult female.—Across the forehead a faint indication of a narrow orange-brown band ; head and hind neck dull brownish-black, the tips of the feathers above the forehead slightly tinged with green, cheeks light blue passing into bluish green on the outer and lower sides of the throat ; a narrow collar on the lower nape, the lower portion of the breast, and abdomen to the vent, bright lemon-yellow ; chest, back, wings, scapulars and their coverts, and the outer sides of the thighs, verditer-green ; the median portion of the apical half of the feathers of the chest slightly tinged with yellow ; rump, upper, and under tail coverts, light verditer-green, the feathers of the latter having a faint yellowish tinge ; primaries black, the apical half of the outer webs of the outermost series grey, the basal half blue ; the remainder blue on their outer webs, black at the tips ; secondaries, black on their inner webs, verditer-green on the outer, the apical half of the inner webs of the last inner secondaries edged and slightly tipped with pale fulvous-brown ; primary-coverts, blue on their outer webs, black on the inner ; lesser, median, and greater wing-coverts, verditer-green, the outermost feathers of the latter passing into a pale verdigris-green ; under surface of the wings and under primary-coverts, black; margins of the shoulders, under wing-coverts and axillaries, pale verditer-blue; two central tail-feathers green, the apical half of the outer webs margined with blue, the next on either side, green, the margins of their inner webs black, the apical half of the outer webs, blue, tipped with bluish-white; the remainder of the feathers green at the base, margined with black on their inner webs, and changing into blue on their outer webs and bluish-white on the apical half of the feathers, the green decreasing and the blue and bluish-white increasing towards the lateral feathers, which are but slightly tinged with green at their base; under surface of the two central tail feathers black, shaded with green on their outer and inner webs for two-thirds of their length, the next on either side black, the margins of the outer webs and the tips bluish-white; the remainder black at the base, light blue on the apical half; bill, bluish-horn colour, lighter at the tip; feet, dark brown. Total length of skin 14·5 inches; wing 6·5 inch; outer tail feathers 4·2 inch; central tail feathers 8·45 inch; bill from forehead 0·9 inch; from nostril 0·7 inch; tarsus 0·8 inch; mid-toe 0·9 inch.

Habitat.—Roeburne, North-west Australia.

Type.—In Australian Museum, Sydney.

Note.—When held in certain lights, the two central tail feathers show numerous bronze cross-bars. Another specimen has the apical half of the outermost secondaries tinged with blue, and the two central tail feathers tipped with black.

Remarks.—Two specimens were obtained by Mr. E. H. Saunders at Karratha Station, thirty-six miles S. W. of Roeburne, North-west Australia, early in 1889, and were referred to by me at the September meeting of the Linnean Society of New South Wales in the same year, as immature specimens of *Platycercus zonarius,* but upon a recent examination of a series of skins of the latter species in different stages of maturity, at present in the Reference Collection, as well as those in the Macleayan Museum at the University, and Dobroyde Collection, I find that the specimens from North-west Australia are quite distinct.

In the disposition of its markings *P. occidentalis* resembles *P. zonarius,* but it differs from that species in having light blue instead of dark blue cheeks; in the greater extent of the conspicuous lemon-yellow of the lower portion of the breast and the whole of the abdomen, *and which extends as far as the vent,* instead of the deep gamboge-yellow of the centre of the abdomen only; in the verditer-green of the chest, back, wings, scapulars and interscapular region, instead of dark green, and in the absence of the narrow black band immediately below the collar.

The SKULL of *DENDROLAGUS DORIANUS*, Ramsay.

By Edgar R. Waite, F.L.S.

(Zoologist to the Australian Museum.)

[Plates XVIII., XIX.]

When examining the Tree Kangaroos in the Museum Collections for the purposes of my paper on *Dendrolagus bennettianus*, de Vis,[*] I was somewhat puzzled by a mounted specimen. As however it did not throw light upon the species under investigation, it was placed aside for future study.

Having once more taken it in hand, I found that it agreed with *D. dorianus*[†] in all described particulars except the non-reversal of the hair. A search among the duplicate collections revealed two other skins, received along with the specimen mentioned; these presented the aspect of the hair peculiar to *D. dorianus*. Another look at the mounted specimen showed that the hair had been brushed in the orthodox manner, namely from head to tail.

These skins were purchased from a Sydney firm of importers in December, 1891, the locality given being the Astrolabe Range, British New Guinea, whence also the types were obtained. One of the skins is headless, but the other contained the skull, from which, however, the occipital region had, as usual, been cut for the purpose of cleaning the cavity.

Dr. Ramsay stated[‡] that in the three original specimens, in the Macleay Museum, "The teeth and all the bones of the skull are in a very bad state, being corroded by the liquid in which the skin was preserved." Baron N. de Miklouho-Maclay[§] supplemented the original description by a more detailed account of the direction of the hair, and by a notice of the teeth as far as could be ascertained from a stuffed specimen.

These further particulars enabled Mr. Oldfield Thomas[‖] to draw up a sufficiently comprehensive synopsis of the cranial

---

[*] Proc. Linn. Soc. N.S.W. (2) ix., p. 571.

[†]   „   „   (1) viii., p. 17.

[‡]   „   „   „   footnote.

[§]   „   „   (1) ix., p. 1154.

[‖] B.M. Cat. Marsupialia, 1888, pp. 94 & 98.

characters; still, in his Catalogue of Marsupials he had to write against the species—"Skull unknown." That this remark may be no longer applicable, is the object of the present paper. Although I have only one skull at my disposal, and that damaged, the mutilation is not of such a character as to interfere with features necessary for comparative purposes.

Dimensions.

Basal length	127·7 mm.
Greatest breadth	78· ,,
Nasals, length	54· ,,
,, greatest breadth	25· ,,
,, least breadth	16·2 ,,
Constriction, breadth	18· ,,
Palate, length	75· ,,
,, breadth outside M^2	37· ,,
,, ,, inside M^2	24· ,,
Palatal foramen	6·8 ,,
Diastema	14· ,,
Basicranial axis	41·7 ,,
Basifacial axis	84·5 ,,
Facial index	206·17 ,,
Teeth, length of I^5	5. ,,
,, ,, P^4	10·5 ,,
,, ,, M^{1-3}	21· ,,

Description.—Skull stout and heavy, sides of muzzle slightly convex. Nasals somewhat expanded behind, their lateral edges concave, narrowest in the middle, posterior suture forming an obtuse backwardly directed angle. Ascending processes of pre-maxillæ greatly and suddenly broadened above, otherwise the pre-maxillo-maxillary suture not greatly inclined. Naso-premaxillary somewhat less than the naso-maxillary suture. Frontal region narrow, immensely swollen, the supraorbital edges sharp and well defined; they are coincident with the fronto-parietal sutures, coalescing where joined by the median frontal suture, thence forming a single prominent sagittal crest to the interparietal. Intertemporal area narrow, little more than the narrowest breadth of the nasals combined, and equal to their anterior breadth. Posterior palate without vacuities. In consequence of the inter-parietal and occipital bones having been removed, their condition, and also that of the foramen magnum cannot be described.

Teeth.—The peculiarities already recorded are generally borne out by this example. I^1 descends much below I^2 and I^1; the two latter are equal in length, I^3 being much the broader. The canine is about three-quarters the length of the smaller incisors and proportionately strong. The premolar has no external ledge and the posterior ridge is deeply notched. The molars are perhaps larger than usual, the cusps very prominent and sharp. The premolar and molar series of the two sides converge before and behind ; the curve continued forward would fall within the anterior teeth. The mandibular premolar inclines very slightly outward. In *D. humholtzi* the incisor lies in a line with the inferior edge of the mandible, whereas in *D. dorianus* it is tilted greatly upwards. Unlike what is found in other species, the ascending rami, and more especially the coronoid processes, converge rapidly above, and are thus accommodated to the very narrow intertemporal area.

A comparison shows that the skull is by far the largest representative of the genus ; the intemporal breadth and the diastema are, however, actually less than in other species.

These points together with the peculiar teeth, the bulging frontals—infinitely more marked than in *D. humholtzi*—the sagittal crest and other features, show that the cranium is as distinct as the external aspect of the animal. The examination of an immature skull only, can show the amount of development the crest undergoes during the lifetime of the animal.

The aggregate characters of the skull indicate a further stage than has been reached by other species in the progress of differentiation from a radical stock.

Note on a Semi-Albino Specimen of *Dacelo Gigas*.

By Alfred J. North, F.L.S.

(Ornithologist to the Australian Museum.)

One of the most interesting of the recent additions to the Ornithological Collection is a semi-albino example of *Dacelo gigas* procured at "Thirribir," Boggabri, New South Wales, by Mr. F. J. Parks during the month of June, and which has been presented by that gentleman to the Trustees. As the bird was received in the flesh and is in perfect plumage, I have taken the opportunity of describing it.

General colour above and below pure white ; a spot in front of the eye, and a broad line extending from the gape to the ear-coverts, dull rufous ; ear-coverts rufous-brown with white shaft-lines ; median portion of the lengthened crest-feathers and an indistinct nuchal spot, dull rufous ; scapulars and interscapular region slightly washed with brown, the lower back faintly barred with brown ; rump and upper tail-coverts dull rusty-rufous, the

former indistinctly barred with silvery-blue, the latter with white ;
tail white, the two centre feathers freckled with dull rufous on
their basal portion and irregularly barred with the same colour
except at the tips ; remainder of the tail-feathers barred alternately with rufous and brown cross-bars for three-fourths of
their length, the bars decreasing in extent towards the outermost
feathers where the rufous bars are entirely lost and the brown bars
become narrow zigzag lines except at the base ; primaries pale
brown, white at the base ; secondaries pale brown, broadly edged
with white on their inner webs ; bastard wing, primary and greater
wing-coverts brown, the innermost series of the latter white ;
median wing-coverts pale brown, the outermost series largely
tipped with white and the innermost series with silvery-white ;
lesser wing-coverts pale brown with whitish tips ; axillaries and
under primary-coverts white, barred with dusky-brown ; remainder
of the under wing-coverts white, narrowly and indistinctly barred
with dusky-brown. Upper mandible brown, the lower fleshy-
white ; iris rich reddish-brown ; legs and feet pale yellowish-
brown. Total length, 17·3 in. ; wing, 9 in. ; tail, 7 in. ; culmen,
2·45 in. ; tarsus, 1·05 inch. Sex ♀ ad., Reg. No. O-8269.

Of the albino specimens of *D. gigas* in the Museum, the finest
example was sent by an unknown donor from Berrima in 1892.
This bird has the whole of the plumage snow-white, with the
exception of one or two of the inner and concealed plumes of the
ear-coverts which are dark brown ; bill dull yellowish-white, with
a few short patchy streaks of blackish-brown ; legs and feet
yellow. In another albino specimen obtained at Bowral, and
presented to the Trustees by the Hon. W. A. Long in 1890, the
only trace of its normal plumage is likewise in the concealed
plumes of the ear-coverts, and in a few brown feathers among
the lesser wing-coverts.

The tendency to partial or total albinism apparently exists
more in this species than in any other Australian bird, judging
by the number of examples represented in the Collection.

In answer to an inquiry of the Curator's asking for further
information regarding this specimen, Mr. Parks writes as follows :
"The semi-albino Great Kingfisher I sent you was accidentally
poisoned by eating mice that had been destroyed by strychnine,
and was found by one of my men. I had been preserving this
bird for some years, which used to feed at the door and nest in
a tree close to the house, and was very sorry when the poor fellow
died ; at the same time I was glad that it was found before it
was too far decayed to preserve as a *rara avis*."

Note on a NEST of *PETRŒCA LEGGII, Sharpe.*

The Scarlet-breasted Robin.

By Alfred J. North, F.L.S.

(Ornithologist to the Australian Museum.)

[Plate XX.]

Mr. Joseph Gabriel, F.L.S., one of the most enthusiastic members of the Field Naturalists' Club of Victoria, has recently forwarded me a beautiful nest of the Scarlet-breasted Robin, built in a very well concealed situation. The nest was found by Mr. Gabriel at Bayswater, Victoria, on the 15th Novr., 1894, and is formed in a small cavity burnt out of the thin stem of a "Mountain Musk," *Olearia argophylla,* at an elevation of about six feet from the ground. The dimensions of this hollow in the stem of the tree, from its base to where it narrows at the top, were six inches and a half in height by three inches and a half in width on one side, and four inches and a half by three inches and a half on the other; and in this snug recess the nest is ensconced. It is composed of very fine strips of the inner bark of a Eucalypt, intermingled with the soft downy covering of the freshly budded fronds of a tree fern, and thickly and warmly lined inside with opossum fur; the rim and one side of the nest are ornamented with cobwebs collected from a burnt tree and to which still adhere small fragments of charred wood, making the nest assimilate closely to its surroundings. On one side of the cavity only a small portion of the rim of the nest is visible. The figure on the plate represents the nest as seen from above and looking into it; as viewed laterally very little of it is discernible. Eventually the nest, which has been presented to the Trustees, and contains three eggs of the usual type, will be mounted and placed in the Group Collection illustrating the life-history of our Australian birds.

The situation of the nest of this species is varied; sometimes it is boldly placed on a horizontal branch or in the forked limb of a low tree, but at all times the exterior portion of the nest is made to closely resemble its environment. In South Gippsland I have frequently found the nest of this Robin by tapping on the hollow trunk of some burnt out giant of the forest, or by watching the bird fly into one of the apertures made by fire in the bole of a large tree.

*DENDROTROCHUS, Pilsbry, ASSIGNED TO TROCHOMORPHA.

By C. HEDLEY, F.L.S.

[Plate XXI.]

FROM considerations of shell characters, and perhaps of geographical distribution, Pilsbry attached † to the genus *Papuina*, a compact and newly defined group, *Dendrotrochus*, embracing the species kindred to *(Helix) helicinoides*, Hombron and Jacquinot. The author of it added that the soft anatomy of the section was unknown to him.

Some examples of the animal of the type species collected by Dr. V. Gaunson Thorp, of H.M.S. "Penguin," presented by him to Dr. J. C. Cox, and transferred by the latter to the Australian Museum, have just been examined by myself. The result is to convince me that at least *T. helicinoides*, and probably the species Pilsbry associates with it, must be dismissed from the genus *Papuina*, and be ranked under the genus *Trochomorpha*. Those features in which *Dendrotrochus* leans from *Trochomorpha* towards more normal Zonitidæ, namely the tripartite sole, caudal mucous pore and side cusps of the rachidian tooth, induce me to hold it as closer than *Trochomorpha* proper to a primitive stock. The evidence furnished by the foot, dentition and genitalia of *Dendrotrochus* harmonise, in the classification I propose, with those characters of its shell which are emphasied in the diagnosis of the section. On page 1 of the work above cited, "columellar margin arcuate, short, not dilated or reflexed," is italicised as an important distinction of *Trochomorpha :* while on page 113, "columellar lip not expanded or reflexed" is given similar prominence in the description of *Dendrotrochus.*

It is a matter of regret to the writer that his inquiries should have led him to mar with corrections a single page of so brilliant a work as Pilsbry's "Guide to the Study of Helices ;" but the progress of knowledge thus exacts its dues as we rise, to paraphrase the poet, on stepping-stones of our dead classifications to higher things.

---

* Since this article was in print, I have received a letter from Mr. Pilsbry, discussing this classification. Accepting the proposed reform, he points out to me that Stoliczka described (*Journ. Asiat. Soc. Bengal,* xlii., Pt. ii., p. 20) a rudimentary tail pore in *Sirella*. From my description he now considers "that *Dendrotrochus* is an arboreal section or subgenus of *Trochomorpha* retaining an old character in the tail pore."

† *Man. Conch.* (2) ix., p. 143.

The detailed description is as follows :—

Animal (fig. 1)—in spirits, with two small left and right mantle lobes, foot in length the shell's diameter, with pedal line, oblique grooves and caudal mucous pore, apparently surmounted by a horn, sole tripartite.

Genitalia (fig. 2)—penis broad, much twisted, containing a large blunt papilla, epiphallus more than twice the length of penis ; vas deferens long, bound to wall of atrium. Spermatheca boot-shaped, duct moderately long. Base of vagina black, lobed, containing no follicles.

Jaw (fig. 4)—rather thin, arcuate, smooth, broad, without central projection.

In a slightly torn radula (fig. 3) I counted $140 = 4 = 12 = 1 = 12 = 4 = 140$ teeth in 103 rows. Rachidian twice as long as wide, basal plate rather hour-glass shaped, central cusp ovate-lanceolate, projecting half its length over the succeeding plate ; small side cusps with distinct cutting points arise at two-thirds the length of the basal plate. Immediate laterals have the entocone suppressed, the ectocone appears as a small hook, the mesocone being broadly ovate. For three or four transition teeth the ectocone rapidly ascends the mesocone, till each of equal size form the bifid cusps of the marginals. These are minute, sinuous, and very numerous.

On a Case of Presumed Protective Imitation.

By Frederick A. A. Skuse.

(Entomologist to the Australian Museum.)

[Plate XXII.]

That wonderful Hepialid, *Leto stacyi*, Scott, seems to claim a place among those famous examples of a similar nature advanced by Bates, Wallace, and others. The protective resemblances among animals is an established fact, and it is unnecessary to quote classical instances. But I cannot find any reference to such a protective feature as that of a moth which resembles *in situ* an approach to the head of a reptile known to possess an appetite for birds. In the case under notice it may fairly be claimed that such an example exists in nature.

After consulting my colleagues, by submitting to them photographs of actual specimens in their natural positions—and I am especially indebted to Mr. Edgar R. Waite, whose opinion, from his special knowledge, is particularly valuable—it was agreed that the moth represented sitting on a tree-trunk forcibly reminded one of the head of the tree lizards, members of the genus *Varanus*. An example is depicted on the plate. It is the "eye" on the wing of the moth that strikes the key-note of the situation ; but in addition the shape of the wing, when the moth is resting, looks very suggestive. The moth is one which passes its larval state in the butts of Eucalyptus trees for the period of five or six years, but on emergence the perfect insect is not prone to fly, and would therefore be very liable to be attacked by birds. Hence the probability that my surmise of the striking resemblance to the head of the lizard being an instance of genuine protective imitation is correct.

The reptile photographed was not very specially selected, and others might perhaps have been used wherein certain features were more strongly marked. For instance, many members of the genus *Varanus* have a dark line passing from the eye backwards.

In conclusion, it might be well to point out that the marks on the outer margin of the visible wing of the moth are very suggestive of labials, while the various lines in front savor of the regularity of scales. Some of these tree-lizards and the moth are natives of New South Wales.

The log from which the moth figured emerged was collected near Newcastle, by Mr. W. Kershaw, late of the Melbourne Museum, and kindly presented to this Museum, thus affording us an opportunity of observing the living moth in its natural position and development.

SOME SUGGESTIONS REGARDING THE FORMATION OF "ENHYDROS" OR WATER-STONES.

BY T. COOKSEY, PH. D., B. Sc.

(Mineralogist to the Australian Museum.)

THE mode of formation of these interesting bodies is still in considerable doubt, and therefore it seems to the writer that these notes attempting to explain their occurrence will not be without interest.

Mr. E. J. Dunn has given a description of the characters of those specimens which he obtained from Spring Creek, Beechworth,

Victoria, and in a later paper in the same volume (page 71) Mr. George Foord more minutely described them, and also gave the results of a qualitative analysis of the liquid contained in one. He found it to be a dilute aqueous solution of chlorides and sulphates of calcium, magnesium and sodium, with a soluble form of silica. The author also sought to explain their formation on the supposition that a certain proportional mixture of colloidal and crystalline silica in solution might have a tendency on deposition to assume a definite crystalline form.

Prof. A. Liversidge, in the Records of the Australian Museum, p. 1 of the present volume, figured and described two large specimens acquired for our Collection, and suggested that they might possibly have been formed by the deposition of silica in hollows or cavities in clay which could have been caused by movements in the clay itself. I have not up to the present been able to find any other literature on the subject, with the exception of references to these bodies as pseudo-crystals, enhydros or water-stones.

A further detailed description is therefore quite unnecessary, but their character may be briefly summed up as follows :—

They consist usually of hollow quartz and chalcedonic formations frequently containing liquid, and are bounded externally by smooth perfectly even surfaces meeting in well-formed sharp straight edges. Some of them from their external appearance might easily be mistaken for true crystals, but a closer examination shews that such cannot be the case, for no two surfaces appear to correspond one with the other. This fact negatives the supposition that they might possibly be pseudomorphs. In some specimens the walls are formed entirely of chalcedony, in others the outer surface only is chalcedonic, while the interiors are either lined or completely filled up with quartz.

Some exactly similar formations were also discovered in Iredell Co., N. Carolina, America, and seven specimens were sent to this Museum labelled quartz-pseudomorphs after calcite. They are exactly similar in every respect to those from Beechworth, Victoria, with this exception, that five of these specimens are composed entirely of quartz, chalcedony appearing to have played no part whatever in their formation. The sizes of the enhydros in the possession of the Australian Museum range from that of half an inch to that of seven and one-eighth inches in length.

Leaving out of consideration for the moment their geometric form, most of these enhydros shew such a striking resemblance to many agates, that one is naturally led to the conclusion that a similar mode of formation must be common to all. Prof. Liversidge's suggestion that they may have been formed by the infilling of cavities in clay, seems to me to fail to account.

* Proceedings of the Royal Society of Victoria, X., p. 32.

for the uniformly flat and even character of the surfaces, and the perfectly straight edges in which those surfaces meet. Mr. George Foord's theory, that a mixture of colloidal and crystalline silica might have a tendency to assume a definite form (that of plates) on deposition is obviously insufficient to account for them, in view of the fact that some of the specimens from America are composed entirely of quartz.

A more probable explanation appears to the writer to be this, that their geometrical form is due to the deposition of chalcedony or quartz on the walls of cavities formed by the intersection of tabular crystals of calcite, the latter having been afterwards removed in solution leaving the enhydros free. The thin septa frequently observed in them are formed in the same manner, the laminæ of calcite being very thin, and the complete specimens in reality a combination of two or more single ones. The occurrence of numerous plates of chalcedony with the enhydros is merely what one would expect, they are, no doubt, broken fragments of similar bodies which were too thin and fragile to retain their original form after removal of the calcite. The exterior surfaces of the enhydros would of course reproduce in an inverted manner those striations, markings, etc., which happened to be existent on the surface of the calcite laminæ, and might therefore lead to the supposition that the chalcedony itself partook of a crystalline character.

On the above assumption the angles between the surfaces of the enhydros must be those between the laminæ of calcite, and some among them would therefore be the same as those known to exist between corresponding surfaces of calcite tables in twin position. From among the numerous angles so formed, several were found to agree, as closely as could be expected from the rough means of measurement at my disposal, with the known angles 127° 29½′, 52° 30½′, 90° 46′, and 89° 14′.

The above view of their formation has been further strengthened by my finding among the numerous mineral specimens in the Museum Collection one in which thin tables of calcite intersect forming geometrical cavities, the walls of which have received a very thin coating of silica. This specimen may therefore be considered as shewing the enhydros in an initial stage of formation. Casts in gelatine taken of a few of these cavities gave forms very similar to those of some of the enhydros.

The latter bodies then, if the above explanation be the correct one, are casts of cavities; and a complete series of them, placed in the position in which they were originally formed, would constitute a mould of those calcite crystals on which the chalcedony and quartz were deposited.

16th September, 1895.

EXPLANATION OF PLATE I.

All the figures refer to *Cerapus flindersi.*

A.—View of a portion of one end of the tube with the animal (a large male) in it, × 9·5.

B.—Dorsal view of the same animal when extracted from the tube, × 9·5. The bases of the antennæ are shown, also a portion of the second gnathopoda and the last pair of pereiopoda; the other limbs being concealed from view. The pleon is bent back under the body. (The front of the head in figures A. and B. has been drawn much too broad.)

a. s.—Upper antenna × 22·5.

a. i.—Lower antenna × 22·5.

gn. 2 ♂ A.—Second gnathopod of large male. × 22·5.

gn. 2 ♂ B.—Second gnathopod of younger male, × 52.

gn. 2 ♀.—Second gnathopod of female, × 90.

prp. 3 ♂.—Third pereiopod of large male. × 52.

prp. 3 ♀.—Third pereiopod of female, × 52.

ur. 1.—First uropod ⎫
ur. 2.—Second uropod ⎪
              ⎬ Seen from above, all × 90.
ur. 3.—Third uropod ⎪
T.—Telson ⎭

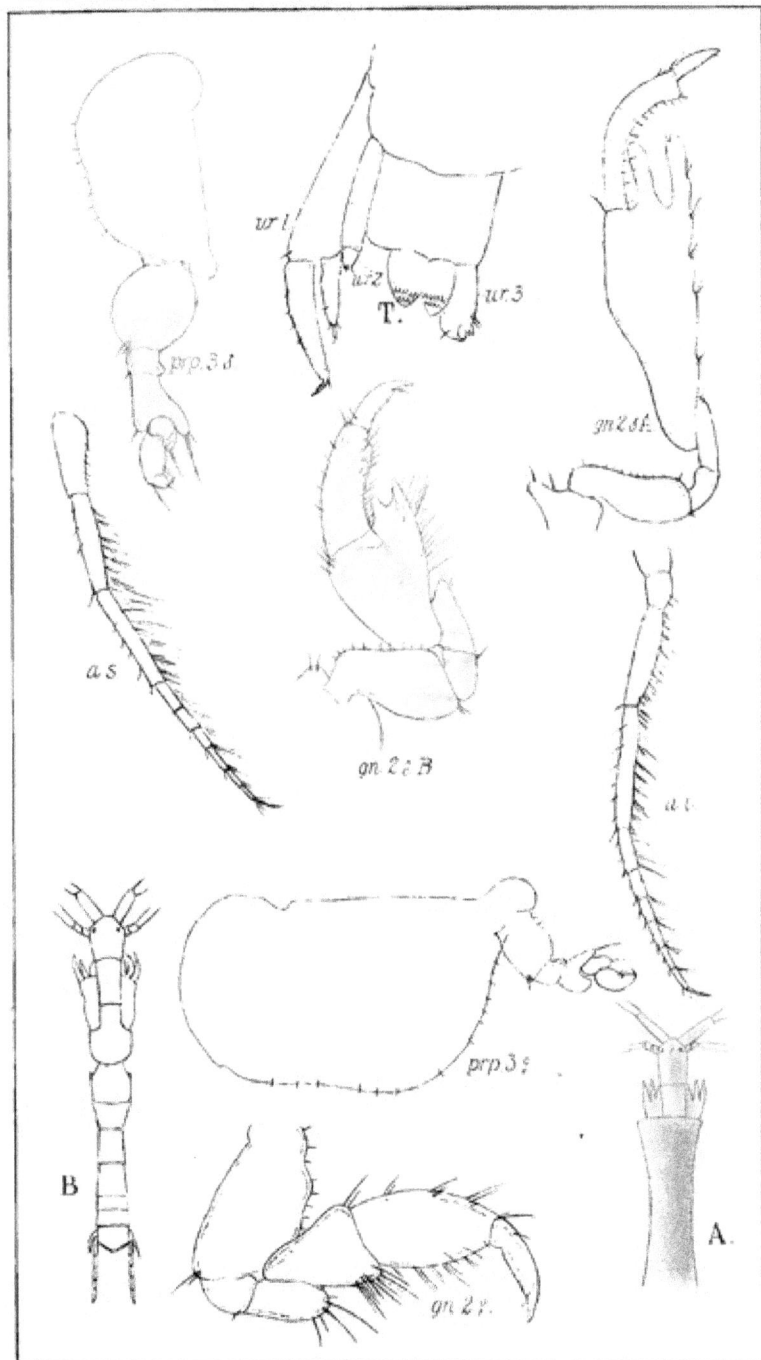

CHAS. CHILTON, del. ad nat.   G. H. BARROW, lith.

EXPLANATION OF PLATE II.

Eggs of the following species.

Fig. 1. *Ninox connivens*, Latham.   Winking Owl.

„ 2. *Calyptorhynchus funereus*, Shaw.   Funereal Black Cockatoo.

„ 3. *Calyptorhynchus solandri*, Temminck.   Solander's Black Cockatoo.

„ 4. *Centropus phasianus*, Latham.   Swamp Pheasant.

„ 5. *Polytelis alexandrœ*, Gould.   Princess of Wales' Parrakeet.

„ 6. *Orthonyx spinicaudus*, Temminck.   Spine-tailed Orthonyx.

The figures are of the natural size.   Reproduced from the originals by heliotype.

EXPLANATION OF PLATE III.

Nest and eggs of *Ptilotis frenata*, Ramsay.   Bridled Honey-eater.

The figures are of the natural size.   Reproduced from the originals by heliotype.

1

5

2

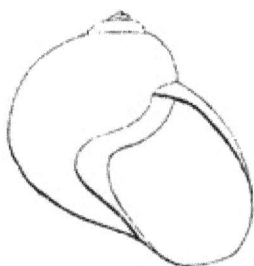

6

3

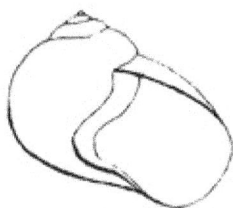

7

4

8

EXPLANATION OF PLATE V.

Fig. 9. *B. kershawi*, Brazier, from the author's type in the Australian Museum.

" 10. Apex of shell of *P. atomata* to show sculpture of embryonic shell, magnified.

" 11. Jaw of ditto, magnified.

" 12. Egg of *Pedinogyra cunninghami*, natural size.

" 13. Genitalia of *P. atomata*.

9

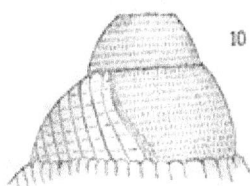

10

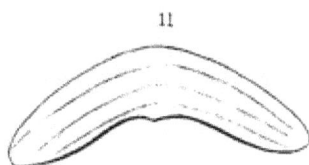

11

12

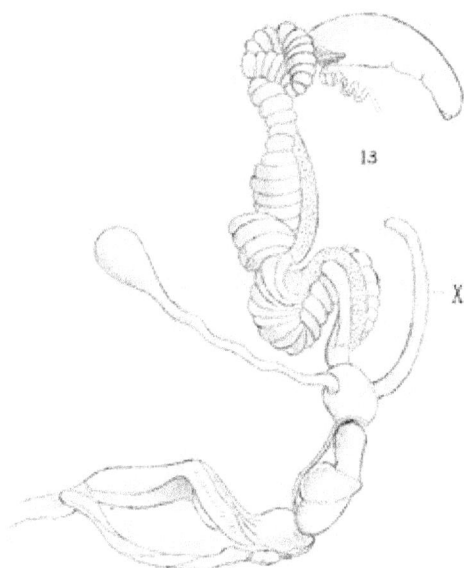

13

X

EXPLANATION OF PLATE VI.

Fig. 14. Two rows of rachidian and immediate lateral teeth from the radula of *P. atomata*, much magnified.

„ 15. Two rows of the 36th to the 42nd teeth from the margin of the radula of the same, much magnified.

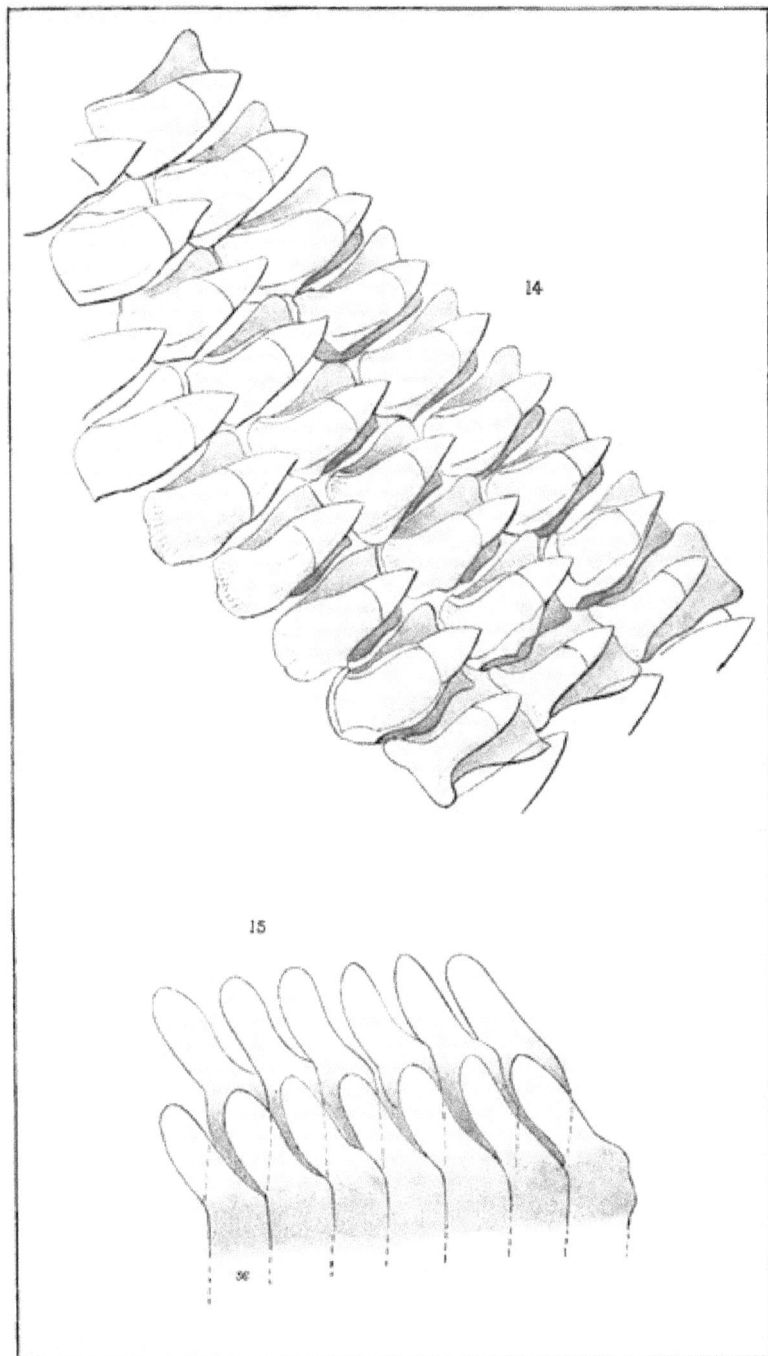

———

Egg of *Manucodia comrii*, Sclater.

Natural size.

EXPLANATION OF PLATE VIII.

CRYSTALS OF MOLYBDENITE, Kingsgate, N.S.W.

Natural size.

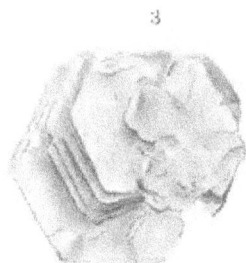

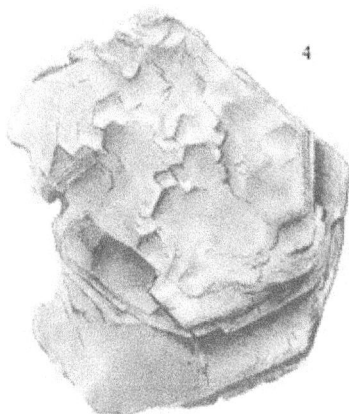

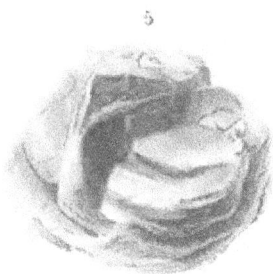

G. H. Barron, del.   Reproduced by the Photoline Printing Co., Sydney

ENHYDRO, OR WATER STONE.

Natural size.

Length, 7½ inches; height, $2\frac{9}{10}$ inches; width, $2\frac{1}{10}$ inches.

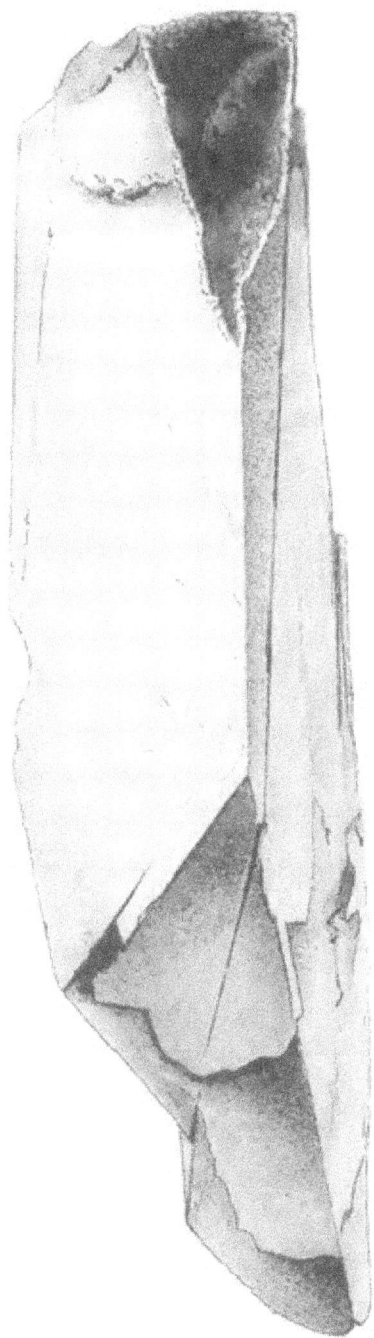

ENHYDRO, OR WATER STONE.

Natural size, foreshortened from a to b.

Length, from a to b, $7\frac{1}{4}$ inches; height $6\frac{2}{3}$ inches; width, $3\frac{3}{10}$ inches.

PLATE X.

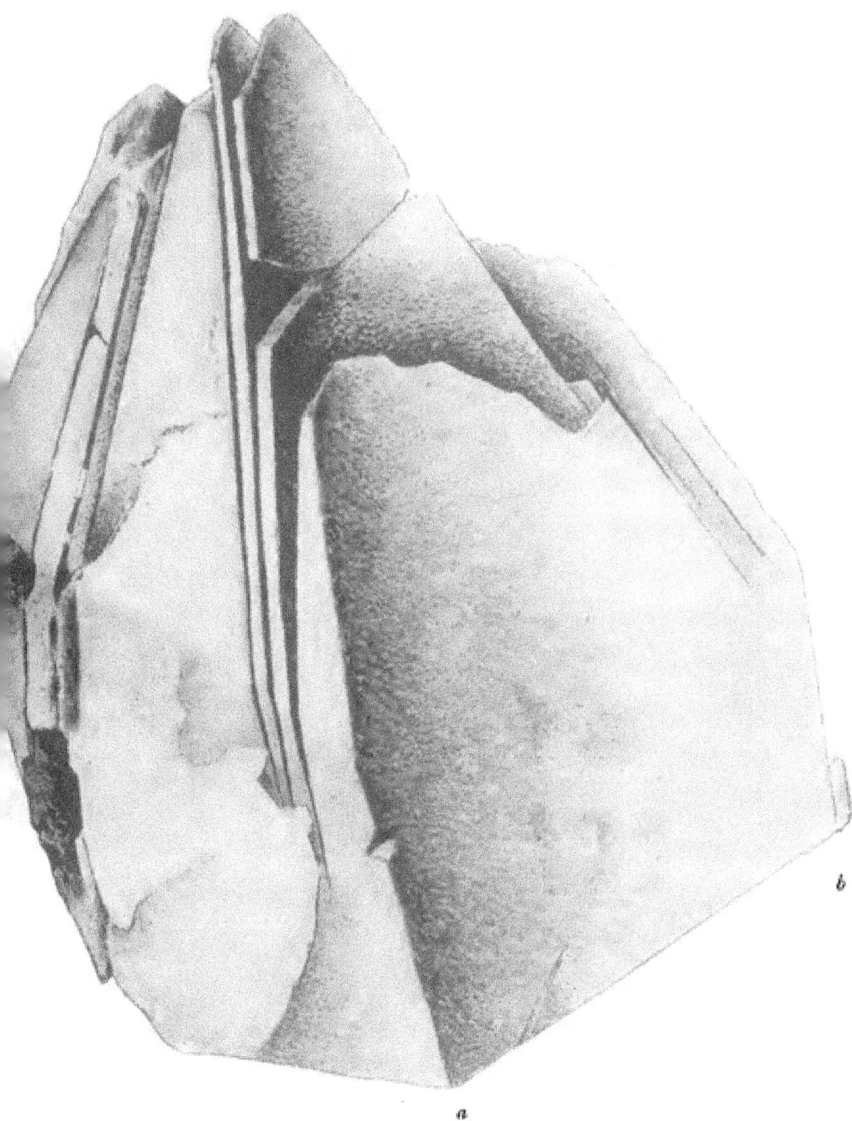

a

b

H. BARROW, del.

Reproduced by the Photoline Printing Co., Sydney.

Fig. 1. *Limnobates strigosa*, Sk., magnified.

" 2. Elytron of same, more magnified.

" 3. *Hydrometra australis*, Sk., magnified.

" 4. *Cyria imperialis*, Don., natural size.

" 5. *Cyria tridens*, Blackb., natural size.

" 6. Right elytron; 7, antenna; 8, 9, and 10, head-parts of same; all
   magnified.

[The figures have been reproduced from drawings by Mr. G. H. Barrow,
of the Australian Museum, by the photoline process.]

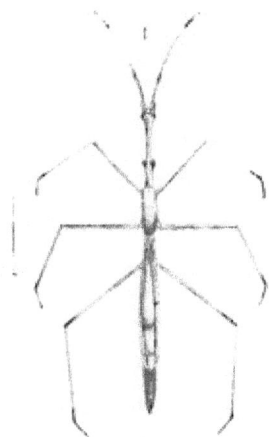

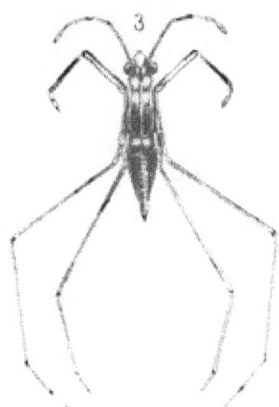

EXPLANATION OF PLATE XII.

Fig. 1. The mass of Hawkesbury Sandstone, known as "Hands-on-the-Rock," Wollondilly River, S.W. corner of the Parish of Werriberri, County Camden.

[Prepared from rough sketches by the Author, by Mr. G. H. Barrow, of the Australian Museum, and reproduced by the photoline process.]

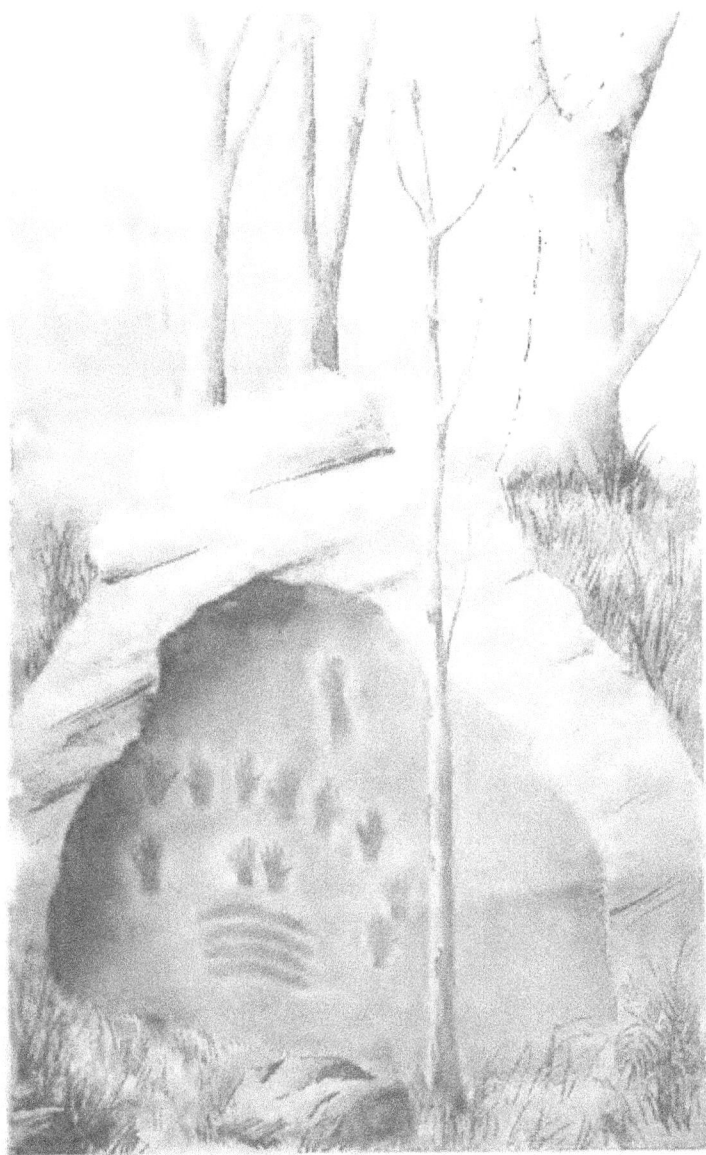

G. H. Barrow, del.   Reproduced by the Photoline Printing Co., Sydney.

EXPLANATION OF PLATE XIII.

Fig. 1. Carved tree *(Casuarina)* near grave, at the "Hermitage," Werriberri Creek, Parish of Burragorang, County Camden.

„ 2. Carved tree *(Eucalyptus?)* near grave, and contiguous to that represented in Fig. 2.

„ 3. Carved tree *(Eucalyptus?)* same localities as those of Figs. 2 and 3.

[Prepared from rough sketches by the Author, by Mr. G. H. Barrow, Australian Museum, and reproduced by the photoline process.]

EXPLANATION OF PLATE XIV.

Figs. 1, 2, and 3. Dorsal, lateral, and ventral aspects respectively of
P. obturamentum.

  ,,   4 and 5. Outlines of *P. similis* to contrast with figs. 1 and 3, copied
from figs. 12 and 14, pl. ciii., Vol. ii., of The Thesaurus Conchyliorum. In the margin of that plate the figures are said
to be " ⅔rds. nat. diam."

[The figures have been reproduced from drawings by Mr. C. Hedley,
of the Australian Museum, by photo-lithography.]

PLATE XIV

1.

2.

3.

4.

5.

EXPLANATION OF PLATE XV.

Figs. 1 and 2. Head of *Typhlops nigrescens*.

  „   3 and 4. Head of *Typhlops proximus*.

Fig. 5. Tail of *Typhlops nigrescens*.

  „   6. Tail of *Typhlops rüppelli*.

[The figures, which are four times natural size, have been reproduced from drawings by Mr. Edgar R. Waite, of the Australian Museum, by photo-lithography.]

1.

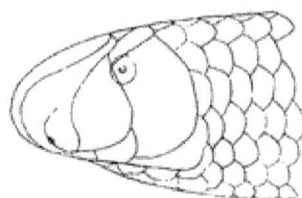

2.

3.

4.

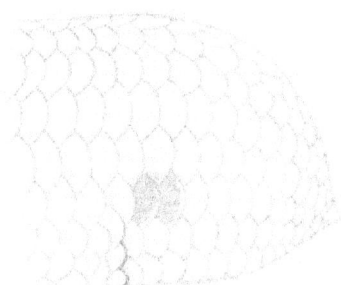

EXPLANATION OF PLATE XVI.

Fig. 1. Large rosettes with small nuclei, and five to eight rings. *Syringo-pora*, Cave Flat.

„ 2. Small rosettes with few rings, a double one to the upper right hand of figure. *Syringopora*, Cave Flat.

„ 3. Smaller rosettes. *Syringopora*, Cave Flat.

„ 4. Surface of *Heliolites*, on the upper right hand both autopores and siphonopores are obliterated, whilst on the lower left hand one of the autopores remains open. Wellington Caves.

[The figures, which are drawn from nature by Mr. G. H. Barrow, have been reproduced by the photoline process.]

1

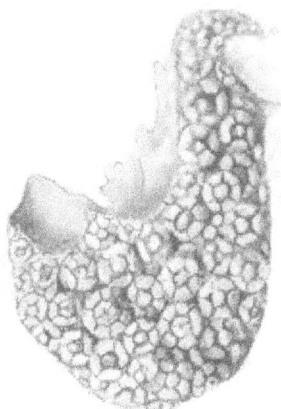

3

2

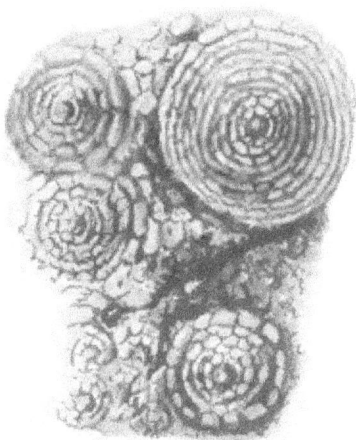

4

EXPLANATION OF PLATE XVII.

Fig. 1. *Stephanocircus dasyuri*, Sk., (male); 1a, head of same; 1b, antenna.

,, 2. *Stephanocircus dasyuri*, Sk., (female); 2a, head of same; 2b, antenna; 2c, maxillary palpus; 2d, fore-leg; 2e, hind-leg.

[The figures, which are all greatly magnified views, have been reproduced from drawings by Mr. G. H. Barrow, by the phot-line process.]

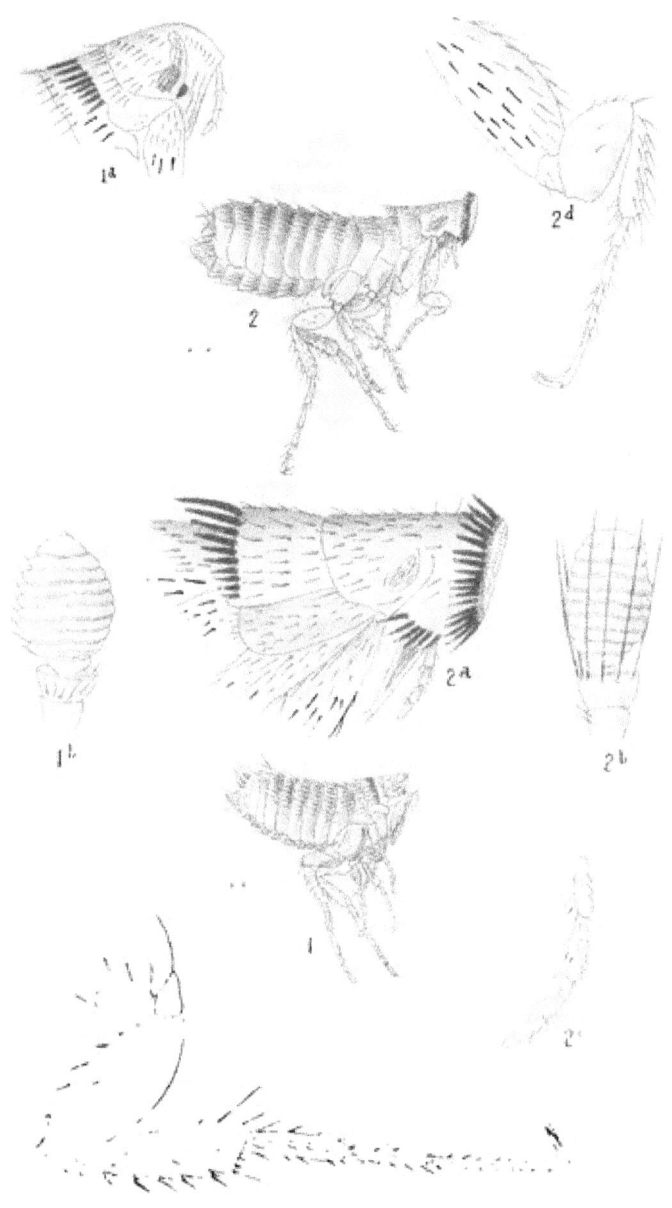

EXPLANATION OF PLATE XVIII.

Dendrolagus dorianus, Ramsay.

Fig. 1. Skull in profile. Natural size.

[From drawings by the Author.]

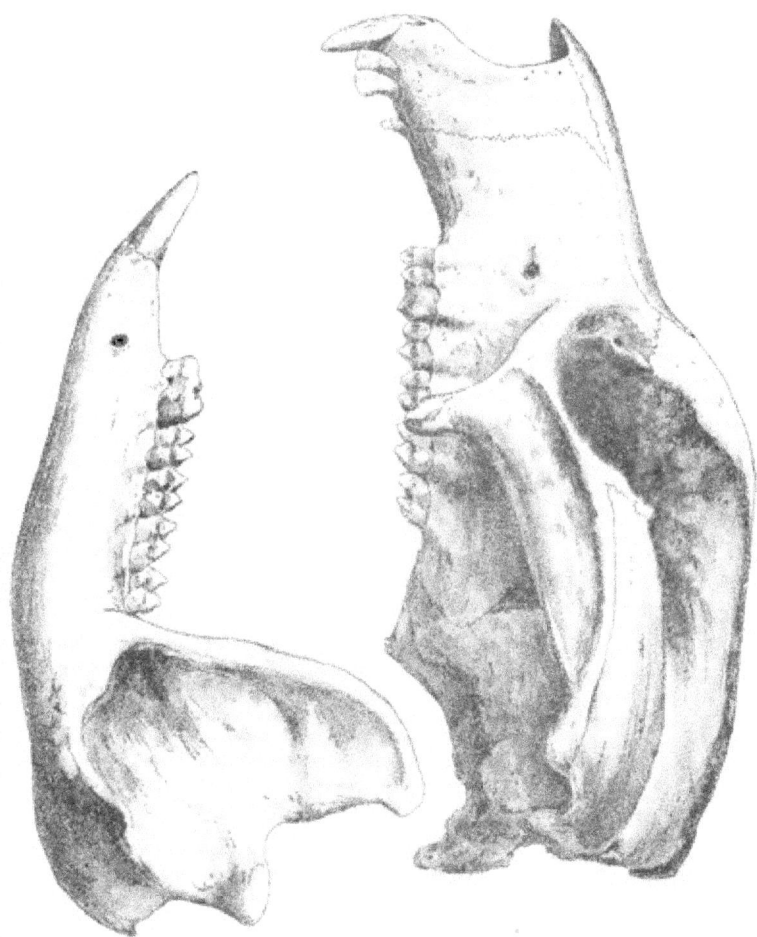

EXPLANATION OF PLATE XIX.

Dendrolagus dorianus, Ramsay.

Fig. 2. Skull from above; reduced.

„   3. The same from below; reduced.

[From drawings by the Author.]

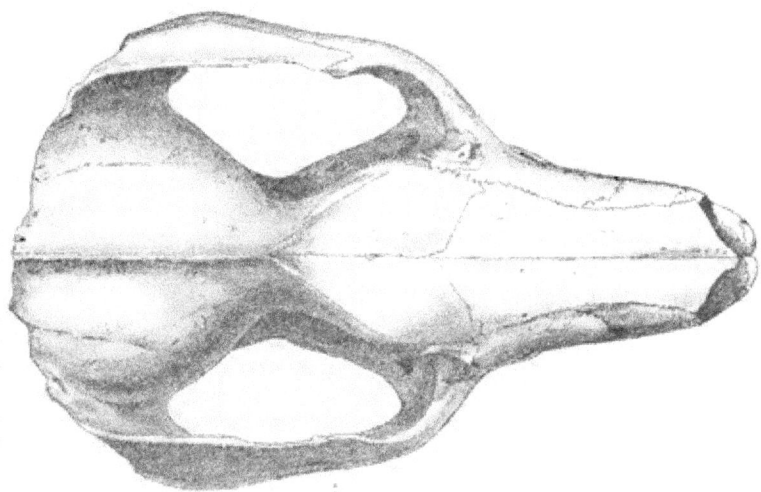

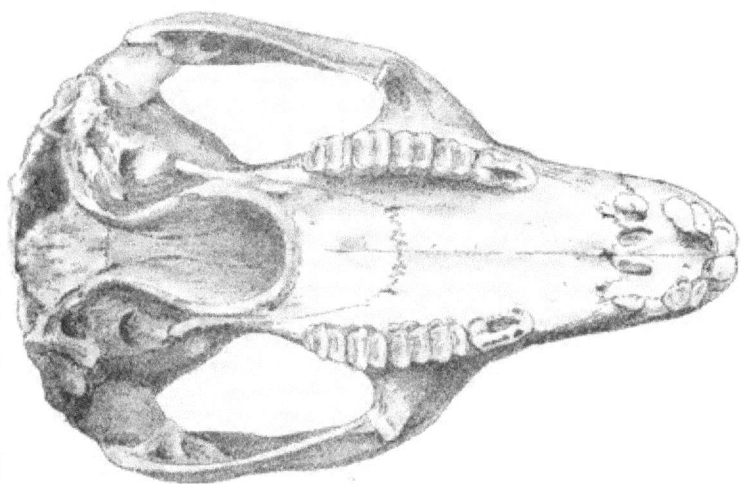

EXPLANATION OF PLATE XX.

Nest and eggs of *Petræca leggii*, Sharpe. Scarlet-breasted Robin.
The plate represents the nest as viewed from above.

Half natural size.

Plate XII

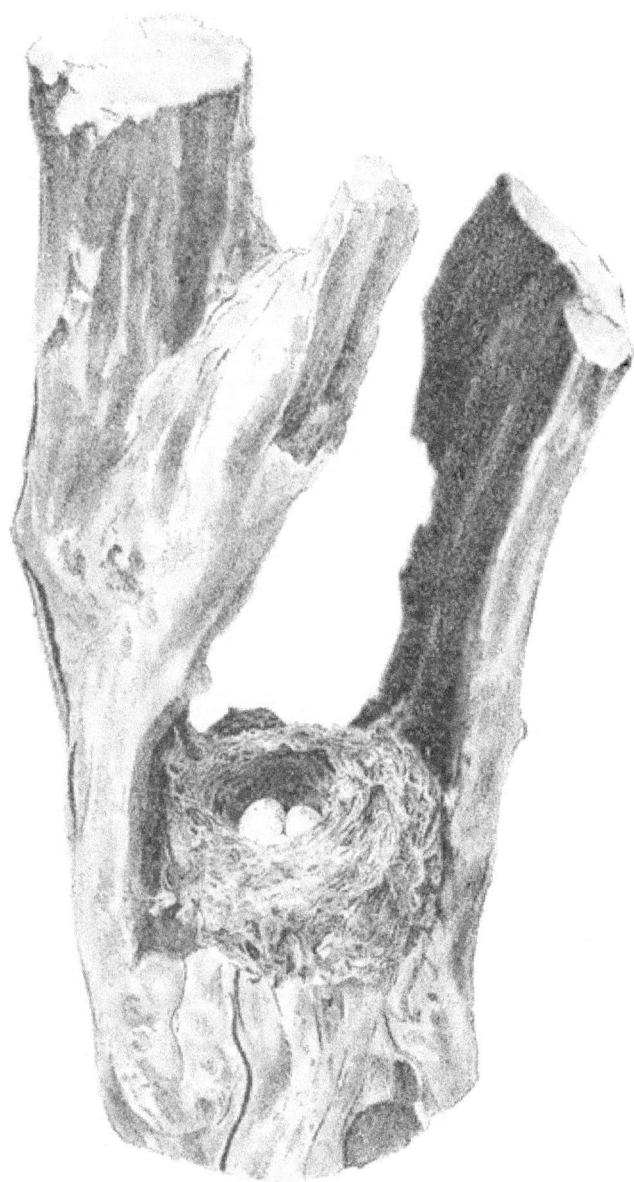

EXPLANATION OF PLATE XXI.

Trochomorpha helicinoides, H. & J., magnified.

Fig. 1. Dead animal extruding from the shell.

„ 2. Genital system.

„ 3. Portion of radula, showing central, transitional and marginal teeth.

„ 4. Jaw.

From drawings by the Author.]

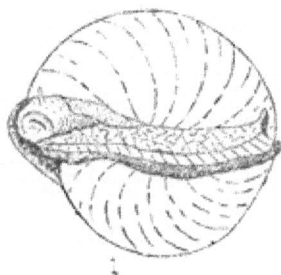

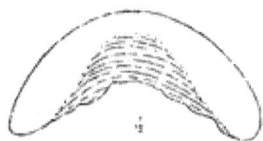

EXPLANATION OF PLATE XXII.

Fig. 1. Head of lizard of the genus *Varanus* on tree trunk.

„ 2. Moth, *Leto stacyi*, Scott, sitting on tree trunk.

Both natural size.

Plate XXII

A MUSEUM ENEMY—DUST.

By Edgar R. Waite, F.L.S.

(Zoologist to the Australian Museum).

Dust is an enemy we are always fighting; every day our rooms are dusted (whether necessary or not !), and once a week, may be, various cabinets containing choice china or other valuable objects are cleared, their contents dusted and replaced. Taken altogether the time occupied in dusting is by no means inconsiderable; to say nothing of the deterioration or danger of damaging the articles of *virtù* so frequently handled.

The principle demonstrated in this essay although thought-out primarily for museum requirements, is alike applicable to general and domestic purposes.

Whilst at the Leeds Museum, I carried out some experiments for Mr. T. Pridgin Teale, M.A., F.R.S., who, at the time, was making observations on dust; more especially with a view to excluding it from cupboards, drawers, &c. As the outcome of these experiments, together with others conducted at his own house and elsewhere, Mr. Teale read a paper before the Manchester Meeting of the Museums Association, entitled—"Dust in Museum Cases, how to battle with it."[*]

The subject is so fraught with interest and importance to all who are in any way connected with museums, that no apology is needed for introducing a matter with which museum administrators have so persistently to contend. It is usually the aim of those who are responsible for the well being of a museum, to make their cases dust-proof; but as Mr. Teale points out, this, by all ordinary methods, is impossible. Air is bound to pass in and out of a case, and why ? because the pressure is always changing; the barometer shows us this ; a rise of the mercury in the tube, indicates that the pressure on our case has been largely increased, and no workman, after these facts have been pointed out to him, will continue to maintain that his fittings will resist a pressure sufficient to burst in the plate glass front. As a matter of fact, the instances are few where the maker claims anything approaching to air-tightness. It will be the experience of most of us, that all except the newest and most modern cases are the very reverse of this. I have myself seen more cases than otherwise, through the chinks of which one could blow out a lighted candle.

---

[*] Report of Proceedings, 1892, pp. 81 – 86.

A sunbeam shows how laden with dust is that atmosphere which otherwise appears so pure ; this suspended dust is forced into a case at every increase of pressure. Before the barometer indicates that the pressure has diminished, and that the surplus air is once more passing out, the dust has probably settled on our specimens and labels ; this interchange of air is going on continually and occurs at least twice daily.   Apart from barometric influences a high thermometer registers a less pressure on the case: a fall in temperature increasing the pressure, forces in dust-laden air at every point of least resistance.

Although museum labels have been referred to as showing the presence of dust, we need not go beyond our own homes for similar indications :—who has not remarked on the streak of dust across a glazed picture, consequent on a minute hole in the papered back or a slightly puckered mount ; the dust track engendered in a book by a crumpled leaf or folded plate ; or again on a dirty ceiling where the position of the non-porous joists is clearly shown by the lighter color of the plaster ?

It has long been known that when air is passed through cotton-wool the dust is filtered out.   Starting with this knowledge, which has been freely applied, Mr. Teale has materially extended our acquaintance with the subject by experimenting with various filtering mediums and showing how such may be used.   It is not my province to recount these experiments ; for such my readers are referred to the paper before mentioned.   The fundamental idea is, to allow air to enter freely through a large aperture, guarded by a filter suitably mounted.   Of those tried, the most effective materials were found to be cotton-wool and cotton-demette.

Our experience at the Leeds Museum was, that very much dust, especially that of a coarser nature, might be arrested by employing such filters.   When first put up they worked admirably, but in time the fibres became clogged with dust.   If not then taken down and brushed, they acted as dust furnishers ; a certain amount being forced through the fibres every time the air passed into the case.

Whilst making experiments in the Australian Museum by the kind permission of the Curator, who also assisted me in every possible way, it occurred to me that the difficulty might be surmounted in another manner :—by endeavouring to protect the case, not from the dust which the pressure forces in, but from that pressure itself.

Adopting the principle of an aneroid barometer, the wall of a case or drawer is to be transformed from an inflexible to a flexible diaphragm, its contained air separated from the air without by an accommodating but impervious membrane ; the ordinary case is porous on account of its immobility.

Such a perfected case may be aptly compared to a piano, the back of which is covered, for acoustic purposes, with a textile fabric ; this has also the secondary and unintentional property of relieving the pressure of air, and guarding the interior of the instrument from the intrusion of dust. There can be little doubt that the efficacy of the filter depends as much upon the flexibility of the material employed, as upon its filtering properties.

In order to put the theory to a practical test, two precisely similar cases were constructed and placed at my disposal. After the joints had been carefully closed, one was fitted with a filter of cotton-demette, and the other with a diaphragm of oiled silk placed on loosely so that sufficient "slack" or "bag" was allowed.

Previous experience had shown that when a filtering material was used, either time or extreme conditions of dust would be required for testing its efficacy. The test cases were supplied with white cards, whereon were placed coins, glass slips and objects designed to register any dust which might be deposited. They were screwed up in August 1894, and placed in the central fish and reptile gallery.

Early in 1895 it was discovered that the roof of this gallery was infested with "white ant" to such an extent that imperative repairs were necessary. This occasioned extreme conditions of dust, and it is not too much to say that the dust created during the removal of the plaster and rotten wood, which process occupied several weeks, was greater than would ordinarily have been formed in many years. The specimens in the two large bird galleries adjoining, which had been screened off, had to be thoroughly cleaned and replaced before the galleries could be reopened, so thickly were they covered with dust. In the light of subsequent events I venture to say, that had the cases been provided with flexible diaphragms, this would not have been necessary.

On opening the test cases (November 1895) in the presence of several of my colleagues, the results were even more conclusive than had been anticipated. Considering the ordeal through which it had passed, the filter had acted well ; the dust deposited was very fine, but sufficient in quantity to show in how far it had failed. To finger one's name on the white card on the floor of the case was an easy matter, but the result was more apparent when the coins were lifted. When magnified, a glass slip resembled, to a non-astronomic eye, a photographic negative of the Milky Way.

On the other case, that is, the one provided with the oiled silk diaphragm, being opened, no trace of dust whatever could be discovered, and when placed beneath the microscope, a glass slip was found to be as clean as when placed in the case fifteen months previously.

The question naturally arises as to whether it is advisable that air in a museum case shall remain unchanged; this is an aspect of the question I do not profess to have studied, but there is one very apparent advantage. In warm climates great trouble is caused by those museum depredators, moths, and particularly the beetles *Anthrenus* and *Dermestes ;* the exhibits have to be constantly handled, and the depredators destroyed. In a case constructed as before suggested, in which no interchange of air takes place, the contained air could be poisoned, and would so remain for a long period.

On the SEASONAL CHANGES in the PLUMAGE of ZOSTEROPS CÆRULESCENS.

By Alfred J. North, F.L.S.
(Ornithologist to the Australian Museum).

In describing *Zosterops westernensis* of Quoy and Gaimard in the " Catalogue of Birds in the British Museum,"[*] Dr. R. Bowdler Sharpe makes the following observations :—" An Australian specimen has been described, and it is extraordinary that a bird which seems to be widely distributed on that continent should so much have escaped notice, the only allusion to the species that I can find in Mr. Gould's work being a passage where he mentions that some specimens of *Z. cærulescens* have the ' throat wax-yellow.' It seems to be the *Z. westernensis* (Q. & G.), a species re-instated in the system by Dr. Hartlaub (J. f. O. 1865) p. 20."

With a view of solving the mystery why so common a species should have been overlooked by most writers, I have given this subject my attention for the past two years, by careful observation and the collecting of a number of specimens of *Zosterops* found in the neighbourhood of Sydney. For a liberal supply of these birds every month, from January until the end of August, the thanks of the Trustees are chiefly due to Mr. H. J. Acland, of Greendale, and for a small series of Tasmanian skins to Mr. E. Leefe Atkinson, of Table Cape. Mr. J. A. Thorpe, the Taxidermist, too, has assisted at various times, and from the specimens

---

[*] Sharpe, Cat. Bds. Brit. Mus. ix., p. 156 (1884).

collected or sent me for examination has prepared a series of nearly fifty skins in every stage of plumage. The result of my observations conclusively prove that the *Z. westernensis* of Quoy and Gaimard, the type of which was obtained by them at Western Port, Victoria, is only the spring and summer attire of *Z. cærulescens* of Latham. Taking the two extreme phases of winter and summer plumage exhibited in *Z. cærulescens*, it can be easily understood why each phase should be thought to belong to a distinct species ; and it is only where one has these birds under daily observation, and obtains specimens during every month of the year that the intermediate stage, or the gradual transition of one phase of plumage to the other, is observed. These changes in the plumage of *Z. cærulescens* have already been pointed out by me in a series of skins exhibited in August last at a meeting of the Linnean Society of New South Wales. Typical examples of Latham's *Z. cærulescens*,[*] with the deep tawny-buff flanks and grey throat, the autumn and winter attire of this species, may be obtained in the neighbourhood of Sydney from the middle of April until the end of August. Some specimens, however, are to be found during April that have not quite lost their summer plumage, and in August others that have already began to attain their spring livery ; these birds have the yellow throat more or less clearly defined. Usually the first indications of losing the deep tawny-buff flanks and acquiring the yellow throat are seen during a normal winter, about the second week in August, in some seasons a fortnight earlier, but in two specimens examined the grey throat was retained as late as the 19th September. During August and September, however, the gradual transition from the winter to the spring attire (the *Z. westernensis* of Quoy and Gaimard),[†] is slowly taking place, and by the middle of October not a bird is to be seen with the deep tawny-buff flanks and the grey throat. Specimens shot in November have the throats of a brighter olive-yellow than at any other period of the year ; the flanks at that time being of a very pale tawny-brown. At mid-summer, when the breeding season with the species is virtually over, the throat is slightly paler than in the spring, and this livery is retained until the beginning of March. The flanks then become darker, increasing in intensity of colour from that time forward, the yellow feathers on the throat also disappearing and passing into grey until the autumn livery is again fully assumed by the end of April.

Of six specimens obtained at Table Cape, Tasmania, during April, 1894, three have the throat grey, the remainder faintly washed with yellow, and in all of them the flanks are of a deeper tawny-buff than in Australian examples.

---

[*] *Z. dorsalis* (Gould). Bds. of Aust., iv., p. 81.
[†] Voy. de l'Astrolabe, pl. 11, fig. 4.

The distinguishing characters in the seasonal changes of the plumage of the under surface of *Z. cærulescens* may be briefly summarized as follows :—

Spring plumage.—Throat bright olive-yellow ; chest and breast ashy-grey, passing into dull white on the abdomen ; flanks very pale tawny-brown ; under tail-coverts dull white, in some specimens washed with yellow.

Summer plumage.—Similar to the spring, but the throat slightly duller in colour.

Autumn plumage.—Throat faintly washed with olive-yellow or gradually passing into grey ; flanks tawny-buff.

Winter plumage.—Chin and sides of the throat dull olive-yellow ; centre of the throat, the chest, and breast ashy ; flanks, deep tawny-buff ; abdomen and under tail-coverts dull white, the latter in some specimens washed with yellow.

Transition from winter to spring plumage.—Throat greyish-white, faintly washed with olive-yellow ; flanks pale tawny-buff ; under tail-coverts dull white, slightly tinged with yellow.

Obs.—The average measurements of examples obtained during winter and in summer are alike. All through the year some specimens are found with the under tail-coverts tinged or washed with yellow. This does not appear to be a sexual character, although from the specimens examined the yellowish wash on the under tail-coverts predominates among the males. As a rule, however, the dull white or white under tail-coverts are found in birds obtained during the winter.

Under the synonymy of *Z. westernensis*, Dr. Sharpe includes *Z. tephropleura*, of Gould, from Lord Howe Island, but the latter species can be readily distinguished from the spring plumage of *Z. cærulescens* by its bright yellow under tail-coverts, and by its larger and more robust bill. At the Macleay Museum I have examined the type of *Z. ramsayi*, described by Mr. George Masters from specimens obtained by him on one of the Palm Islands, lying north of Halifax Bay, N.E. Queensland. It is a good and distinct species, with olive-yellow under tail-coverts, and a broad zone of white feathers round the eye. Dr. Sharpe, from the description of this species given in the Proceedings of the Linnean Society of New South Wales,* considers it probably identical with *Z. westernensis* ; but there is no question that the specific character pointed out by Mr. Masters, and the olive-yellow under tail-coverts will prevent one when examining this species from confounding it with the spring or summer plumage of *Z. cærulescens*, or with any other Australian member of this genus.

---

* Vol. i., p. 50.

NOTES on MOLLUSCA from the ALPINE ZONE of MOUNT KOSCIUSKO.

By C. Hedley, F.L.S.

(Conchologist to the Australian Museum).

[Plate XXIII.]

The Alpine fauna and flora have elsewhere yielded such interesting results that it is with pleasurable anticipations a student turns to the consideration of this chapter in Australian Biology. The restricted developement of high land here holds out, however, no promise of a rich harvest. In Australia the alpine zone is almost limited to the plateau of Mount Kosciusko, an elevation so insignificant (7,256 ft.) that on other continents it would rather be termed a hill than a mountain.

Two observers have contributed, especially to our knowledge of the physical features of this district. In January, 1885, Dr. R. von Lendenfeld made a brief reconnaissance and under the titles of "Meteorology of Mount Kosciusko" and "The Glacial Period in Australia" communicated some of his experiences of it to the Linnean Society of New South Wales. A more detailed account of his travels appeared as a Parliamentary Paper, Sydney, 1885, and in Petermann's Mittheilungen, 1887.

Later, several visits, the first under the auspices of this Institution, were paid by Mr. Richard Helms. In a "Report of a Collecting Trip to Mount Kosciusko,"* in an essay "On the recently observed evidences of an extensive Glacier Action at Mount Kosciusko Plateau," † and in a paper now being published by the Royal Geographical Society of Australasia, N.S.W. Branch, he has recorded observations on the geology and natural history of the district. Considerable zoological collections were formed by Mr. Helms, which have not yet been exhaustively investigated.

"An isopod of a very old and greatly generalised type,"‡ he procured at the 5,700 level, was described by Dr. C. Chilton§ as *Phreatoicus australis*; a species since collected at the 4000 ft. level on Mount Wellington in Tasmania and which completes a genus of two other species from South New Zealand. This distribution supporting that of *Geonemertes australiensis*, Dendy,‖

---

* Rec. Austr. Mus. i., pp. 11-16.
† Proc. Linn. Soc. N.S.W. (2) viii., pp. 349-364.
‡ Thomson, Trans. Linn. Soc., Zool. (2) vi., p. 301.
§ Rec. Austr. Mus. i., pp. 149-171.
‖ Proc. Linn. Soc. N.S.W. (2) x., p. 372.

and Tasmanian types of Orthoptera and Coleoptera* suggests that the alpine fauna of Mt. Kosciusko is primarily or specifically Tasmanian and secondarily or generically Antarctic. This generalisation accords perfectly with the mollusca I am about to discuss. The Tasmanian colony left stranded on the Kosciusko heights demands a former cold period to explain their existence there as clearly as does a moraine left by a vanished glacier. Had not geologists furnished evidence of an Australian Glacier Epoch, then biologists would have had to invent on their own account a theory of such.

As the molluscan collection has not reached me whole, these observations make no pretence to exhaust the subject, the interest attending which justifies the publication of data, however fragmentary. On the return of Mr. Helms from his first trip to Mt. Kosciusko, a single species of his molluscan captures was at once entrusted to me, though not then engaged in the Museum service, for description. This was an unfigured species, then only recorded as Tasmanian, which I identified,† with some hesitation from insufficient data as *Cystopelta petterdi*, Tate. These doubts were dispelled ‡ afterwards by an examination of living specimens in their type locality. Since then, this species has been traced in Victoria to Ballaarat (Musson), and Loch, (Frost): in New South Wales to the Kurrajong Hills (Musson), Mount Wilson (J. C. Cox), and Blackheath (Quaife).

On resuming the examination of the Kosciusko mollusca five years afterwards two new species first claimed my attention.

EDODONTA NIVEA, *n. sp.*

(Plate XXIII., Figs. 5, 6, and 7).

Shell, white, thin, small, shining, flattened, involute, and perforate. Whorls, three, closely coiled, the earlier enrolled within the latter and almost concealed by them. Spire, a shallow crater, one third of the shell's major diameter, from the floor of which the whorls centrifugally ascend. Umbilicus, narrow, one eighth of the shell's major diameter, a hollow screw showing the revolutions of two whorls. Sculpture, last whorl perpendicularly crossed by 115 sharp costae diminishing in size and approaching one another at the suture and umbilicus ; on the vertex and base the interstices, from three to five times the breadth of the intervening costae, are crossed by minute spiral raised hair lines forming meshes which are in turn crossed by three or four most minute longitudinal threads ; in the peripheral zone the spiral

---

* Op. cit., iv., p. 398.
† Proc. Linn. Soc. N.S.W., (2) v., pp. 34-40, pl. i.
‡ Op. cit., vi., p. 24.

lines are evanescent. The penultimate whorl has 61 costæ. The first whorl is spirally grooved. Aperture oblique, lunate ovate, lip deeply incurved at the suture, rising above the vertex, arched above and below, not thickened and scarcely reflected at the columella. Inner lip overlaid by an opaque granular callus burying in its advance the costæ in its path.

Diameters, major $3\frac{1}{4}$, minor $2\frac{3}{4}$, height $1\frac{1}{4}$ m.m.

Loc.—Wilson's Valley, at an altitude of 4,500 ft., Mt. Kosciusko, N.S.W. (Helms).

Type—Australian Museum, C. 67.

This species nearly approaches *E. antialba*, Beddome, from Tasmania, from which its narrow umbilicus and shallow spire readily distinguish it. Other species compared by their respective authors to *E. antialba* are *E. subantialba*, Suter, from New Zealand, and *E. amula*, Tate, from Central Australia; besides other differences both are much smaller than that now introduced.

FLAMMULINA EXCELSIOR, *n. sp.*

(Plate XXIII., Figs. 2, 3, and 4).

Shell large for the group (subgenus *Flammulina*), turbinate, spire rather elevated, thin, translucent, surface dull, barely perforate, whorls three, rapidly increasing, last flattened above, rounded at the periphery and ventricose on the base. Suture impressed, coloured on a pale ground by angular brown flames of irregular pattern, usually most distinct at the suture and fading away both at the periphery and on the penultimate whorl, frequently directed downwards and forwards they cross the growth lines diagonally and breaking up about the periphery produce a mottled pattern. Sculpture, close irregular growth lines commence as coarse wrinkles at the suture and fade into the smooth base, faint spiral scratches are seen under the microscope to cross these; the earliest whorl exhibits regularly spaced costæ crossed by fine spiral striæ. Aperture oblique, ovate, lip sharp, the somewhat twisted columella is folded over a minute perforation; a thin granulated callus is spread over the inner lip and curves around the umbilical region. Diameters, major 9, minor 8, height 6 m.m.

Loc.—Pretty Point, at an altitude of 5,700 ft., Mt. Kosciusko, N.S.W. (Helms).

Type.—Australian Museum, C. 71.

This very fragile shell of a group hitherto unrecorded from Australia seems in shape to be nearest allied to *F. cornea*, Hutton, from Auckland, New Zealand, from which its size, colour, and perforation distinguish it. In a bottle with *Cystopelta*, but without locality more precise than "Victoria," Prof. W. Baldwin Spencer has sent me examples of this species in spirits. The foot, white dotted with black, showed a tail gland and papilla, parapodial grooves and oblique furrows.

Other species brought by Mr. Helms, from Mt. Kosciusko, were:

ENDODONTA TASMANIÆ, *Cox.*

Ref.—Cox, Mon. Austr. L. Shells, p. 22, pl. xii., fig. 4 (3 figs.); Petterd, Mon. L. Shells Tasmania, p. 31, etc.

Loc.—Pretty Point, at an altitude of 5,700 ft., Mt. Kosciusko. This is the first record of the species occurring outside Tasmania.

ENDODONTA PARVISSIMA, *Cox.*

Ref.—Cox, in Legrand, Collections Mon. Tasm. L. Shells, species 39, Pl. ii., fig. 1 (3 figs.); Petterd, Mon. L. Shells Tasmania, p. 22.

Loc.—Pretty Point, at an altitude of 5,700 ft., Mt. Kosciusko. Like the preceding not hitherto known beyond Bass Straits. Doubtfully identified from insufficient material.

ENDODONTA TAMARENSIS, *Petterd.*

Ref.—Petterd, Journ. Conch. ii., p. 213; iii., p. 175 (as *H. rosacea*), Mon. Tasm. L. Shells, p. 30; Tate, Proc. Roy. Soc. S.A., iv., p. 75; Billinghurst, Victorian Naturalist, 1893, p. 62; Hedley, Proc. Linn. Soc. N.S.W., (2) ix., p. 43.

Loc.—Wilson's Valley, at an altitude of 4,500 ft., Mt. Kosciusko. From Launceston, Tasmania (Petterd), it has been traced to Burrumbeet (Tate), Mount Franklin (Billinghurst), Victoria; and Blackheath, N.S.W. (Quaife). In the last locality it was associated with *Helicarion verreauxi* and *Cystopelta petterdi*, both fellow emigrants from Tasmania.

ENDODONTA ALBANENSIS, *Cox.*

Ref.—Hedley, Proc. Linn. Soc. N.S.W., (2) vii., p. 163, pl. ii., f. 5-8; Proc. Malacol. Soc. i., p. 260.

Loc.—Pretty Point, at an altitude of 5,700 ft., Mt. Kosciusko. Specimens collected by Mr. C. T. Musson at Tamworth, N.S.W., and presented to the Museum represent the most northern point known to be attained by this species.

ENDODONTA FUNEREA, *Cox.*

Ref.—Cox, Mon. Austr. L. Shells, p. 16, pl. iii., f. 1.

Loc.—Moonbar (3,500 ft.) and Wilson's Valley (4,500 ft.), Mt. Kosciusko. Ranges from S. Queensland to Victoria.

DESCRIPTION OF PUGNUS—HEDLEY. 105

ENDODONTA PARADOXA, Cox.

Ref.—Cox, Mon. Austr. L. Shells, p. 31, pl. xi., f. 13 (as
H. morti), etc.

Loc.—Moonbar (3,500 ft.), Mt. Kosciusko. The form here
recorded is larger and more globose than typical examples.

CHLORITIS BREVIPILA, Pfeiffer.

Ref.—Pilsbry, Man. Conch., (2) vi., p. 265, pl. lviii., f. 29-30.

Loc.—Moonbar, Mt. Kosciusko, N.S.W.

Mr. Helms also reports a Paula, from Mt. Kosciusko, probably
P. atomata, Gray, which has not come into my hands.

RHENEA SPLENDIDULA, Pfeiffer.

Ref.—Pfeiffer, Conchylien Cabinet, (2nd ed.), Band I., Abth.
12, pt. 2. p. 109, pl. lxxxv., f. 1-3.

Loc.—Mt. Kosciusko. East coast of Australia generally.

DESCRIPTION OF PUGNUS, A NEW GENUS OF RINGICULIDÆ, FROM SYDNEY HARBOUR.

By C. HEDLEY, F.L.S.

(Conchologist to the Australian Museum).

[Plate XXIII., Fig. 1.]

Among several microscopic shells taken by Mr. A. U. Henn
on stones at low water in Little Manly Cove, near Sydney, one
attracted our special attention. The finder gratified the writer
by placing the novelty in his hands for study, and on learning
the result thereof has generously presented to the Australian
Museum the most perfect of the three specimens obtained, which
constitutes the subject of the present communication.

The long narrow aperture was contrasted in turn with every
involute shell figured in Pilsbry's Monograph of the Order* without matching it. Then it occurred to me that those features of the
thickened lip, etc., in which the new form departed from the plan
of Cylichna, Tornatina, and so on, were all characteristic of
Ringicula, whose very different outline had not at first invited
attention. Critical comparison enforced the conviction that a
telescoped Ringiculoid had now presented itself; for which a

---

* Manual Conch., (1) xv., pls. 18 - 60.

vague resemblance to the palmar aspect of a clenched left hand suggested the name of,—

PUGNUS, *gen. nov.*

By its thrice folded columella, anterior canal, thickened outer lip, and sculpture of spiral grooves crossed by transverse striæ, this very distinct genus takes a place in the family Ringiculidæ. From the only other surviving genus *Ringicula*, *Pugnus* is separated by its involute shell and buried spire. In the shortness of the spire the Cretaceous fossil *Avellana* occupies a position intermediate between these two. Its contour is however more globose, and those subordinate groups which agree with *Pugnus* in possessing a smooth lip, appear to differ by having one columella plication only. The type and only species is,—

PUGNUS PARVUS, *sp. nov.*

Shell minute, white, solid, oblong, involute, spire buried, imperforate at either extremity, the posterior of the inner portion of the last whorl obliquely sloped. Sculptured by about thirty spiral grooves, whose interstices are three times their breadth, and are cut by longitudinal striæ into squarish facets. Aperture as long as the shell, vertical, contracted in the middle, expanded anteriorly and posteriorly, inner lip overlaid with callus ; outer lip smooth, greatly thickened externally and internally, springing from a false umbilicus in the vertex, arched higher than it, arcuate peripherally, curving below the whorl up to the columella and channelled at the junction ; anteriorly the columella bears a strong entering fold, posterior and parallel to which is a weaker one, and posterior to this again a small deeply-seated third fold is just distinguishable. Length, 1½ ; breadth, 1mm. Animal unknown.

Loc.—Manly, near Sydney, alive, at low tide on rocks, and dead in shell sand from Middle Harbour. (A. U. Henn).

Type.—Australian Museum, C. 2524.

———

DESCRIPTION OF A *DAPANOPTERA* FROM AUSTRALIA.

By FREDERICK A. A. SKUSE.

(Entomologist to the Australian Museum).

———

In the present contribution it appears advisable that it should be prefaced by an explanation of the reason why scientific names and descriptions, which the majority of the public does not seem to quite understand, are published in the manner they are, and why such a course is necessary to the end for which they are written.

It is frequently asked "Why do you naturalists put long-winded Latin or Greek names to your specimens?" "Why not do so in plain English?" This is, however, not so easily complied with as may be imagined, and where done, it is in many cases, only calculated to mislead. Popular names are usually bestowed upon objects existing in nature by local consent and usage : that is by the folk inhabiting the particular district or region where the animals, plants, or whatever else they may be, exist ; and these names convey to them, only, perhaps, an idea of what is meant. Professor Bell, a celebrated authority on British Crustacea, visiting a seaport town, enquired at a fishmonger's stall, on which was a plate of crabs for sale, whether that particular kind of crabs was eaten in the locality? With great surprise at his apparent ignorance, the reply came, "They ben't crabs, sir ; them's *spiders !*" But to come nearer home. What is ordinarily known in Sydney as the "lobster" or "crayfish" is really a crawfish, recognised in science as *Palinurus Huegeli* and throughout the world as such. So that what is called a "lobster" by many people, will be known by the name of "crawfish" or "crayfish" by some, and maybe a dozen other local appellations by as many others to whom the identical animal may be familiar. But lobsters, crawfish, and crayfish are totally distinct from each other in structure and with different habits. And thus it is that mistakes happen in giving names to animals which to the popular eye exhibit a more or less fanciful resemblance ; but in many other cases there is not the slightest likeness or even affinity. What are commonly styled "locusts" in this country are really *Cicadæ*, belonging to a totally distinct and widely separated order of insects. And, moreover, the same kind of *Cicada* is known by different names in different localities, such as " Miller," " Mealy-back," etc. The true locusts belong to the grasshoppers, whilst the Homopterous Cicadidæ have been known as "Cicadas" from times of remote antiquity. Instances such as these may be multiplied, but those cited should be sufficient to demonstrate the uselessness of the adoption of local names for the purpose of general information.

Popular names, if general, would be of great advantage in assisting to gain a scientific knowledge of the objects themselves, but they rarely can be said to assist specialists in their investigations for the public weal in this respect. And herein lies the secret. Specialists of all nationalities must compare notes as to the affinities and geographical distribution of the objects under investigation, in discussing their properties and utility. In order to attain this end, it is absolutely necessary to adopt an universal language as the medium for exchanging ideas before the result of their combined researches can eventually be made popularly intelligible in different languages. To this end Greek and Latin are employed.

The Tipulid hereafter described is intimately related to those species included in the genus *Limnobia*—in fact it is a modified *Limnobia*. The only tangible differences occur in the wings. The genus *Dapanoptera* was proposed by Osten-Sacken in 1881 for four species previously described by Walker under the title *Limnobia*,[*] which had been collected in New Guinea and the neighbouring islands by Wallace. Osten-Sacken points out[†] that, "The peculiar, although only secondary character, upon which this genus (*Dapanoptera*) is established, is found in the wings, which being deeply colored, have a conspicuous hyaline spot at the end of the first longitudinal vein ; upon reaching this spot the first vein becomes abruptly evanescent ; both its ends (that is the cross-vein, running towards the costa, and the real end of the first vein turned towards the second) are placed within that hyaline spot and are colorless and very weakly marked, sometimes imperceptible. The known species have a *supernumerary cross-vein* in the first posterior cell, beyond the discal (a great deal beyond in *D. plenipennis*, and only a little in the other species.)" The wing of *D. plenipennis* also greatly differs from the other known species in being conspicuously undulatory on its posterior border and in having the second and third longitudinal, and also the first vein issuing from the discal cell, strongly undulatory. *D. richmondiana* appears to agree very well with the remaining three species in general plan of venation and regularity of contour of the wing ; with antennæ, male forceps, dentate claws and the auxilary vein as in *Limnobia*.

The discovery of *Dapanoptera* in the tropical jungle of northern New South Wales adds another interesting instance to the numerous evidences of a former Papuan invasion ; and, in passing, the occurrence of *Libnotes* may also be mentioned. To quote Hedley,[‡] "The types encountered by a traveller in tropical Queensland (and also northern New South Wales), or rather in that narrow belt of tropical Queensland hemmed in between the Cordillera and the Pacific, all wear a foreign aspect. Among mammals may be instanced the cuscus and tree kangaroo ; among reptiles, the crocodile, the *Rana* or true frog, and the tree snakes ; among birds, the cassowary and rifle birds ; among butterflies, the *Ornithoptera ;* among plants, the wild banana, orange and mangosteen, the rhododendron, the epiphytic orchids, and the palms ; so that in the heart of a great Queensland 'scrub,' a naturalist could scarcely answer from his surroundings whether he were in New Guinea or Australia." And he adds, " It may be supposed that late in the Tertiary epoch, Torres Straits, now only a few fathoms deep, was

* Journ. Linn. Soc. Zool. v., p. 230, (1861) ; vii., p. 202, (1864) ; viii., pp. 103, 104, (1865).
† Studies on Tipulidæ, ii., Berl. Entom. Zeits., xxxi., p. 178, (1887).
‡ Proc. Austr. Assoc. Adv. Sci., Adelaide, v., p. 445, (1893).

upheaved, and that a stream of Papuan life poured into Australia across the bridge so made."

As aptly remarked by Osten-Sacken, the species of *Dapanoptera* "are the birds of paradise among the Tipulidæ, the more so as they come from the home of the true birds of paradise."

Order DIPTERA.

Family TIPULIDÆ.

Dapanoptera, *Osten-Sacken.*

DAPANOPTERA RICHMONDIANA, *sp. nov.*

♂ and ♀   Length of antennæ .... 0·063 in... 1·60 m.m.
Expanse of wings... 0·380 x 0·098 in... 9·60 x 2·40
Size of body .... 0·279 x 0·048 in... 7·50 x 1·20

Bright ochreous yellow. Head, rostrum, and palpi black; antennæ brown, fourteen-jointed; first joint of the scapus twice the length of the second; flagellar joints twice as long as broad, verticillate-pilose. Thorax more or less tinged with brown at the sides, and sometimes with the indication of a median stripe; pleuræ sometimes brownish beneath the bases of wings. Club of halteres brownish. Abdomen more or less distinctly brown or blackish above, especially the last segments; male forceps with a distinct adminiculum; female ovipositor slightly curved, ochreous. Legs long, the femora sooty or dark brown at the tips.

Wings concolorous with the body and legs, with two brown patches: a hyaline stripe starting between the bases of the sixth and seventh longitudinal veins and widening to the middle to the anal cell between the fifth and sixth, terminating at the first brown patch; and an elliptical hyaline spot at the end of the first longitudinal vein; the first brown patch extends from the costal to the posterior margin of the wing, it is widest between the costa and the fourth vein and abruptly narrower in the second basal cell, from whence it again widens to the border; the second patch is roundish, wider than the first, occurs before the tip of the wing and encloses the discal cell, and the white elliptical spot at the tip of the first longitudinal vein occurs about midway between its sides. Auxiliary vein reaching costa opposite the distal end of præfurca which is very angularly bent; subcostal cross-vein rather long, close to the tip of the auxiliary; first longitudinal vein (and cross-vein) evanescent or very pale above the hyaline spot; supernumerary cross-vein (in first posterior cell) situated a little beyond the discal, great cross-vein before the middle of the latter; sixth longitudinal vein nearly straight.

Hab.—Dunoon, Upper Richmond River, N. S. Wales (Helms). Three specimens in March.

STEPHANOCIRCUS, Sk.: A REJOINDER.

Mr. Carl F. Baker omitted to include a diagnosis of my genus in his table of the genera of the Pulicidæ* as he evidently first wished to "verify all the points of the description" by the examination of actual specimens. I would explain that the flea in question was taken in large numbers on one animal, *Dasyurus maculatus*, Kerr, and that there is no mistake in attributing the two sexes figured in my paper† to one species.‡ It would possibly not conform with Mr. Baker's preconceived system of classification of what he calls "Siphonaptera." Before essaying the task of reconstructing existing classification it is usual for the reformer to make himself acquainted with the literature bearing on the subject. Mr. Baker, however, discusses my conclusions at second hand and without attention to the numerous figures upon which I relied to elucidate my meaning. Under these circumstances it is scarcely fair in him to condemn my article as confusing together two species referable to known genera. What genera they should be referred to, Mr. Baker, exercising more discretion than valour, fails to indicate. It is at least remarkable that one supposed species should be all males and the other all females. Were such the case they might produce a hybrid in consonance with Mr. Baker's classification.

There is a tale extant of a conchologist who elaborated a classification of Mollusca; one shell however, which refused to fall in line with his system was promptly disposed of under his heel, to save further trouble. It would appear that my *Stephanocircus* merits a similar sad fate.

In conclusion I might mention that a very remarkable flea was described from Australia§ by Olliff, under the name of *Echidnophaga ambulans* (from the peculiar character of its inability to jump), but no notice is taken of this insect in Mr. Baker's papers.

F. A. A. SKUSE.

---

* Canad. Entom., xxvii., p. 68.
† Rec. Austr. Mus., ii., p. 77, pl. xvii.
‡ Strong evidence is furnished by Mr. Baker, himself, when he affirms (l.c., p. 132), "It is not a usual occurrence for two species of fleas to be found living together on a single wild animal," that there is no error in my data.
§ Proc. Linn. Soc. N.S.W., (2) i., p. 172, (1886).

MINERALOGICAL NOTES.

By T. Cooksey, Ph.D., B.Sc.

(Mineralogist to Australian Museum).

1.—Precious Opal from White Cliffs, N.S.W.

On examining a cut and polished specimen of a fossil-bearing ferruginous sandstone boulder from White Cliffs, N.S. Wales, I was struck by the appearance of the precious opal which had replaced the carbonate of lime of the shells. The rock is permeated with the opal, and particularly when polished has a very beautiful appearance. The minute surfaces in the interior of the opal which produce the play of color, when viewed with a lens, appear to be quite flat and terminated by perfectly straight edges often parallel. On a closer examination under the microscope with reflected light, the appearance in many places was strikingly similar to that of a section of crystalline marble viewed with crossed nicols. The light and dark banded appearance due to twinning in the marble was perfectly imitated in the opal and on rotating the specimen on the stage the bands became alternately coloured.

As the play of colour in the opal is produced by minute cracks in its substance, the planes of colour seen by reflected light are therefore produced by cracks which apparently occupy the same position as the cleavages of the calcite displaced by the opal; occasionally the traces of cleavages could be seen distinctly on one of the bright surfaces and the angles formed by their intersection were approximately those found in calcite. Other portions again showed a somewhat fibrous structure. In many places on focussing into the substance of the opal these cleavage planes could be distinctly seen, and the rhombic forms produced by them were so exactly similar to those obtained by cleavage in calcite that a doubt as to their origin seemed out of the question.

From the above observations it is evident that the carbonate of lime of which the shells were originally composed had first been converted into crystalline calcite (by which all shell structure had necessarily been lost), and then the calcite replaced by opal. The latter had also reproduced the cleavages of the former, and it is these that cause the play of colour which gives to the opal its precious character. Cracks or fractures of a conchoidal form are also present and also produce colour by reflected light but the brilliancy of the specimen for the most part results from the presence of these characteristic cleavages.

2.—Basic Sulphate of Iron from Mount Morgan.

A specimen supposed to have been a fossil bone was sent to this Museum for examination and identification by Mr. R. L. Jack, Government Geologist for Queensland, he having received it from Mount Morgan.

Mr. Gibb Maitland, Assistant Government Geologist for Queensland, writes me that this and similar specimens were found in Number 11 Floor, Freehold South Stopes, thirty-eight feet below the surface of the ground. They occur in a matrix of oxide of iron, the latter forming a dyke, eighteen feet in width, dipping to the north-east, and consist of nodules of all conceivable shapes and sizes, surrounded by iridescent oxide of iron, manganese, and other auriferous clayey matter.

Mr. Jack expressed the opinion that their origin was not organic, which was subsequently confirmed by the Curator of the Australian Museum. A superficial examination of the specimen in question supported this view, and determined it to be a concretion of a basic sulphate of iron containing alkalies. On the strength of this result, Mr. W. R. Hall presented to the Trustees of this Museum the specimen already received. It seemed to me that a more exact determination of the nature of the body would be of interest.

Properties.—To the naked eye the specimen appears a compact mass of a dull brown colour weathered slightly on the outside to a yellow powder. The powdered substance itself has a yellow colour, and under the microscope is seen to consist of minute crystals. It is but very slightly soluble in water, but completely soluble on boiling for a short time with hydrochloric acid. Heating in a tube causes a liberation of acid water and the substance on cooling turns red. Before the blowpipe it turns black, becoming highly magnetic, and slightly fuses on the edges. Its specific gravity is 3·107.

An analysis gave the following percentage composition—

$$
\begin{array}{ll}
H_2O & = 9\cdot96 \\
Fe_2O_3 & = 49\cdot13 \\
Na_2O & = 4\cdot43 \\
K_2O & = 3\cdot88 \\
SO_3 & = 33\cdot31 \\
\hline
& 100\cdot71
\end{array}
$$

No water was given off by heating the powdered substance to 175° C. for two hours. The above percentage for water was obtained by heating a weighed quantity to dull redness for a short time, noting the loss of weight, and then estimating the quantity of SO_3 left in the residue. From these numbers and the known total of SO_3 in the substance the amount of water was calculated.

By extracting twice with boiling water, 0·8% was dissolved, which contained a trace of chloride, probably salt.

The specific gravity and the analysis, with the exception of the proportion of potash to soda, agree very closely with those given by Dana in "A System of Mineralogy," p. 975, for *Jarosite*, but the insolubility in water of the Mount Morgan mineral seems to show that the two bodies cannot be identical. The latter body is, without doubt, derived from the decomposition of pyrites.

January, 1896.

EXPLANATION OF PLATE XXIII.

————

Fig. 1. *Pugnus parvus*, Hedley.

Figs. 2, 3, 4. Various aspects of *Flammulina excelsior*, Hedley.

„ 5, 6, 7. Various aspects of *Endodonta nivea*, Hedley.

[All magnified, and to various scales, drawn from types by the Author.]

1

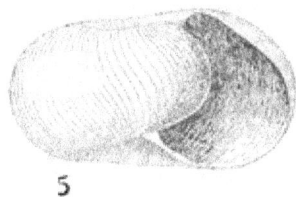

5

2

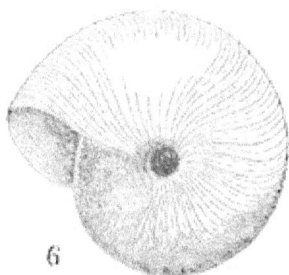

6

3

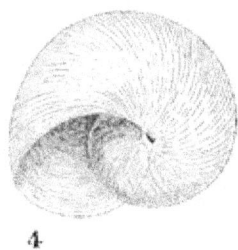

4

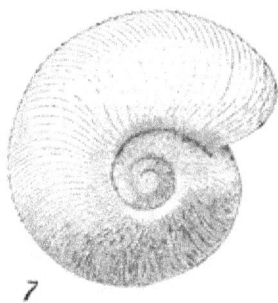

7

INDEX.

www.ingramcontent.com/pod-product-compliance
Lightning Source LLC
Chambersburg PA
CBHW030820270326
41928CB00007B/818